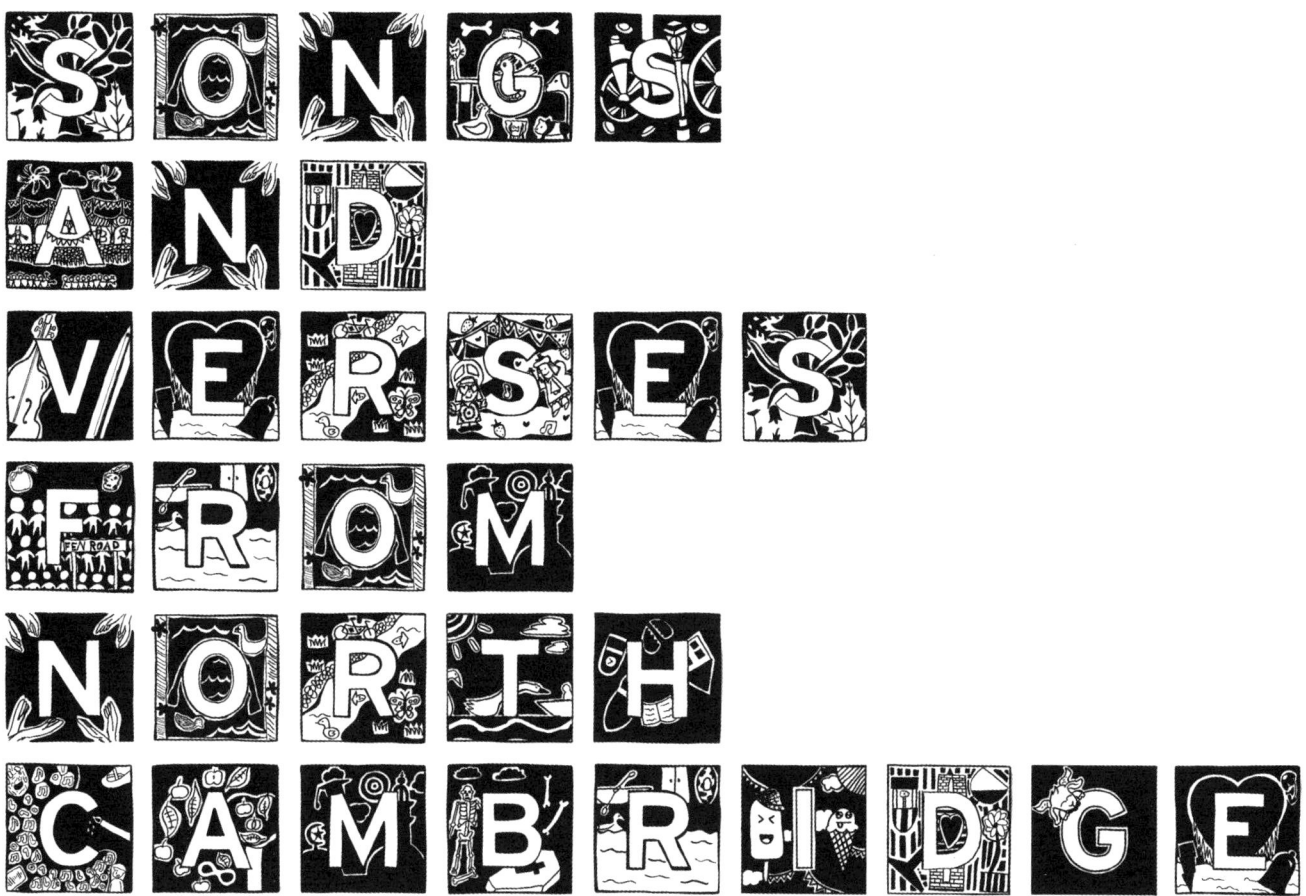

Songs and Verses from North Cambridge

By Emily Peasgood and

The North Cambridge Community

Published by: Emily Peasgood, Rubber Chicken House,
2 Kent Place, Ramsgate, Kent, CT11 8LT
www.emilypeasgood.com

Cover art and letters by the children of Chesterton Community College
Design and music transcription by Emily Peasgood
Illustrations, typesetting and map by Danielle Woolley
Printed by Ex Why Zed

ISBN 978 1 8382219 0 4

 ABLE OF CONTENTS

8   Foreword By Commission Projects

9   To Lose My Writing By Abigail Thorne-Miles

10 Introduction By Emily Peasgood

12 This Book Is Free By Emily Peasgood

13 Song & Verse Notes

14 16 Chesterton Road

16 A Battle Of Plates

18 Arbury Carnival

20 Arbury Court

22 Beth Shalom

24 Big Issue

26 Black Fen Club Blues

28 Boathouse

32 Burial No.4

36 Cambridge Community Arts

38 Chesterton Allotment Society

40 Chesterton Waltz

42 Dating In CB4

46 Eliza

48 Fen Road

- 50   G.O.A.T.
- 55   Map Of Songs & Verses
- 58   Green End Road
- 60   Grumpy's Pet Shop
- 62   Halifax Road
- 64   Heron Man
- 66   Kindness Is Always In Season
- 68   NHS Clap
- 70   River Shanty
- 72   Seasons
- 76   Steamroller Park
- 80   Strawberry Fair
- 82   The Ballad Of Mr Asbo
- 86   The Ghost Of The Snowcat
- 88   The Sharing Shelf
- 90   The Summer Of 1989
- 92   Turin The Python
- 94   Union House
- 98   When Daisy Met Winston
- 102   When Jonny Plays
- 104   Acknowledgements
- 105   The Songwriting Team
- 106   Chesterton Community College Artwork
- 108   Licence

 OREWORD BY COMMISSION PROJECTS

Songs and Verses from North Cambridge is the latest of an ongoing series of art projects commissioned by Brookgate. It continues their commitment to carefully considered and strategic contributions by artists to the development process, informed by site, and of benefit to both existing and new communities.

Led by Emily Peasgood, the project marks an important new departure involving musicians and local people in the creation of new music that celebrates north Cambridge. Brookgate are proud of this approach and hope that this commitment to developing innovative ways of working sets a precedent.

The production of this songbook is the culmination of a year-long programme of activities by Emily and her team whose long experience of creating music with communities has had exemplary results. The 34 songs and verses by contributors from the many communities across north Cambridge contributes to a legacy which it is hoped will be built on.

It is remarkable that much of the project was undertaken during COVID 19 'lock down' and it is a tribute to its leadership that it was possible to develop ways of delivering the programme when contact became impossible.

Projects of this kind rely on the valuable input of others and the initial work by Network Rail, the support of the Cambridgeshire Library Service and input of the staff and pupils of Chesterton Community College have been particularly valuable.

Songs and Verses from North Cambridge marks an important point in the development of north Cambridge, contributing to this exciting new district and encouraging new interests and skills amongst the community. We hope that this will continue.

David Wright
Commission Projects

O LOSE MY WRITING

When words and stories are not recorded, they are eventually lost in time. This book captures and preserves local stories for future generations. Abigail shares the importance of doing so, and how she would feel if her writing was lost forever.

To lose my writing; the feeling of knives cutting up my soul the same way life has cut through my confidence; completely desolating my being in this life. All my heartbreak would have been for nothing. My ethos; without heartbreak: there is no art. Without art there is no gaiety for the lost souls being cut with those same knives used to obliterate human beings from the ones they love. Writing; my one, true love. I can only begin to imagine the annihilation that has hacked a place in the hearts of those whose writing is lost from their identity. To all those who spoke the beautiful words of Cambridge many years ago, I am wholeheartedly apologetic for the loss of who you truly are. The soul has been sliced out of your city. To lose my writing would feel nothing but heartbreak. Your lost words brings great sadness, to not only my heart, but to the hearts of your entire city.

By Abigail Thorne-Miles

INTRODUCTION

As a young musician, gigging around folk clubs in Grimsby, I would scour the local library for songs I could perform. When I found 'The Singing River' by John Connolly and Bill Meek (1985) I fell in love with the songs about local people and places in Grimsby, Hull and the River Humber. They captured what it was like to live in South Humberside in the 1980s and have stayed with me throughout my life. As my career has developed, I have moved towards creating musical compositions that are installed as sound installations in historic public places. But there is always a hint of my folk roots in my work, from my interest in working in the community to the melodies I write and the stories I tell.

I jumped at the chance to create an artwork with people in north Cambridge. The brief centered on the CB4 postal area comprised of: Arbury, Chesterton, Kings Hedges, Orchard Park, Cambridge Business Park and Cambridge North train station. It was an area undergoing significant development and change, and I wanted to know what it was like to live there and what made this area unique. I hoped to capture the sense of place by creating songs that explored urban myths, mysteries, characters and landmarks while preserving local stories for future generations to enjoy.

This work references the British Folk Song Revival of the early 20th century which saw folk song collectors like Cecil Sharp, Lucy Broadwood and Ralph Vaughan Williams recording and notating folk songs with local people in rural communities. At the time, these songs were kept alive by passing them from person to person by word of mouth. They changed and evolved as time passed and it became impossible to know the original author. They were rarely recorded for posterity, and sometimes disappeared into obscurity along with the stories they told. At the dawn of the 20th century, the folk song collectors sought to preserve what was becoming a vanishing oral tradition and captured the words and music of local people to create musical resources for future generations. Many of the songs collected in the revival form the canon of folk music performed today. This project aims to have a similar effect by capturing stories from north Cambridge for future generations to perform and enjoy.

'Cambridge North Folk Song Project' was conceived and I organised songwriting workshops, which were to be opened by the greats of British folk music. A big performance of the songbook was planned and a preview was booked at Cambridge Folk Festival. However, with the events of 2020 our plans were cancelled and replaced with online songwriting sessions, one-on-one. I reached local people in the only ways available to me: social media, community groups, local radio stations and word of mouth. Together, this helped to spread the word. Cultural organisations and Cambridge City Council were instrumental in helping me to reach a diverse group of people from many different backgrounds and age groups. Our youngest songwriter is 8 years old and our eldest is in their 80s. I was fortunate to be supported by a fantastic songwriting team: Anna Hester Skelton and Bob Hines. For a year, we met with up to twenty people a week. We developed rapport, explored ideas and eventually, created these songs and verses.

I hoped to celebrate as many facets of life in north Cambridge as possible, and as people started to sign up, the project expanded to include spoken word, rap and other genres of music considered outside of the realm of folk music. I questioned if this material could be in a folk song book, and what 'folk music' is today. Many of the songs performed by contemporary folk musicians were collected in the folk song revival or are inspired by historical artefacts and verses in ballad books. While folk music has evolved to expand its use of instrumentation and features, there is still an aesthetic quality that we instantly recognise as folk music. I believe these sounding qualities are rooted in the songs and music collected during the folk song revival;

that folk music today contains sonic resonances of the music collected 100 years ago. The work of the folk song collectors has lived on for 100 years, has evolved into a tradition of its own and is a testament to the importance of capturing stories and music with local people.

Folk music is more than the preserved notations and recordings folk song collectors made 100 years ago. It moves beyond a specific sound and into social contexts. Folk music contains stories shared in local communities, which change as they pass from person to person, breathing new life into songs and melodies which evolve and grow. Today, folk music references the culture it is created in and takes many forms. Folk music is music of the people.

This project took place in the north of Cambridge with a diverse group of local people whose stories might have otherwise been lost. Some contributions were made independently or anonymously, and the majority were developed with the songwriting team. All contributions were included. While some authors are professional writers and musicians, the majority have not written a song or verse before. My team and I took great efforts to facilitate ideas without changing them into something unrecognisable. The resulting book reflects the culture and musical styles of people in north Cambridge communities in the early 21st century. I hope that everyone who uses this book finds a song or verse they can relate to, and I hope they will still be performed in 100 years. Only time will tell.

Some of the songs in this book echo the tradition of folk music and others take a different form like pop song Dating in CB4, rap song Steamroller Park and house music piece Heron Man. As the transcriber and arranger, representing this musical diversity in the form of musical notation was a challenge. I approached Heron Man and Steamroller Park by notating the individual rhythmic, melodic and harmonic components and inviting people to create their own arrangement on acoustic or digital instruments. Flexibility is a theme throughout this book: you are encouraged to interpret its contents freely and to adapt and arrange it to suit your needs. Apart from G.O.A.T. and Green End Road, the songs and verses in this book can be used freely in any way and no licence or fee is required. The only requirement is that you credit the authors as detailed in This Book Is Free!

I couldn't be prouder of this book and of the efforts of those who contributed songs, poems, ideas, stories and most importantly, time. This project has taken me back to my roots and to the importance of celebrating people, places and stories that might be forgotten in the passage of time. The culmination of Cambridge North Folk Song Project forms a body a contemporary folk songs and verses that capture a moment in time in a community that is evolving and changing. It celebrates and explores locations, events, places, organisations, personal stories, daily life and local histories. I hope the community spirit recorded in this book will still be around in 100 years. This community song and verse book contains stories that capture what it was like to live in north Cambridge in 2020. Here are just 34 of them. Please sing the songs, read the verses and remember their stories - that is why they were written.

Emily Peasgood

Lead Artist & Composer

Cambridge North Folk Song Project

 HIS BOOK IS FREE

By Emily Peasgood

Copyright is an important feature in the lives of artists and musicians. Our ideas are our only currency and in my practice, I fiercely protect my copyright. Creating this book raised many challenging ideas around copyright, particularly as one of its primary aims was to create freely available songs and verses that would survive because people didn't have to pay to perform and record them. It is unsurprising that many British community music groups and performers draw from the canon of folk songs collected in the revival. As part of an oral tradition, it is impossible to trace the authors of these songs and they are public domain; anyone can perform and record them and they can be adapted with ease. The traditional folk songs we know and love today have survived for this reason. This book embraces the nature of public domain songs and eschews copyright by setting its contents free to evolve as time passes and to increase the likelihood that they may still be known in years to come.

The people who contributed ideas, stories, songs and poems did so freely and generously to create a community song book available free of charge for the public to access and enjoy. Ideas and material were given anonymously, independently or collaboratively for this purpose. Following the completion of this book, song and verse contributors assigned their copyright to me, in order that I could make waive my rights and make the totality of the book freely available. There are two exceptions: G.O.A.T. by Lucille Rococoa and Green End Road by George Bacon. These pieces were not written as part of this project but capture the story of the local area and the authors have kindly given permission for them to be included in this book. All other songs, verses and accompanying illustrations can be performed, adapted, edited, rearranged, photocopied and recorded by anyone and no licence or fee is required. However, the moral rights-the right to be credited-of the writers for each song and verse are upheld. If a song or verse is used in any way, the writers should be credited; the authors of the works contained in this book have asserted their rights to be identified as authors in accordance with sections 77 and 78 of the Copyright, Designs and Patents Act 1988. The licence for this book is available to view on page 108. I hope you will take as much pleasure from this book as I had creating it with the people of north Cambridge.

# SONG & VERSE NOTES

The way these songs are interpreted is entirely up you. Most songs are notated simply with a melody and chords and block lyrics. Others have more specific notation and instrument suggestions, or complement specific performers. For ease of use, some suggestions of suitability for specific groups or contexts are provided below - but again, these are only suggestions as each song can work in different ways.

The songs and verses have an original intention and a way the author created them to sound. Sometimes, there is an accompanying performance suggestion at the top of the score. However, in all cases what you see is a guide. You are encouraged to interpret songs with flexibility. Rearrange and adapt them, change the order of sections, alter the pace, change the chords, rewrite the melody or tweak the lyrics. Anything goes.

A CAPPELLA SOLO SINGER: Black Fen Club Blues and Fen Road.

CHILDREN'S SONGS: Arbury Carnival, A Battle of Plates, Grumpy's Pet Shop, NHS Clap (with recorder), The Ballad of Mr Asbo and Turin the Python (recorder).

CHOIR AND MULTIPLE SINGERS: Beth Shalom (round song), Burial No. 4 (backing vocals and round song), Fen Road (round and part song), River Shanty (call and response with improvised harmonies) and Union House (3-part song).

DIGITAL INSTRUMENTS: Heron Man (house music), Steamroller Park (rap, song and GarageBand samples).

INSTRUMENTAL: Chesterton Waltz.

SINGER-GUITARIST/PIANIST OR BAND: 16 Chesterton Road, Arbury Court, Big Issue, Boathouse, Cambridge Community Arts, Chesterton Allotment Society, Dating in CB4 (pop), Eliza, Green End Road, Halifax Road, Kindness is Always in Season, Strawberry Fair, The Ghost of The Snowcat, The Sharing Shelf, When Daisy Met Winston and When Jonny Plays.

SPOKEN WORD: G.O.A.T, Heron Man, Seasons, Steamroller Park and The Summer of 1989.

To listen to the author's demos of the songs and verses visit:

emilypeasgood.com/songs-and-verses-from-north-cambridge

# CHESTERTON ROAD

"This song is inspired by a building near my house that has been shut for some time. It looks back at its history and how it has served the local community since it opened in the 1920s. There is an optional interlude that can be performed before or after each verse. The rhythm can be interpreted freely to allow for breathing."

Deborah has lived in Cambridge since 2017 and works at the University of Cambridge. She enjoys playing music in her spare time, sings in Cambridge Rock Choir, and hopes this building will be a cinema again one day.

By Deborah Slee
and Emily Peasgood

(Lyrics)

1. By the Boat-house on Chesterton Road there's a building, It's all painted white and surrounded by hoardings, for several years now the whole place has been closed, and the birds have been nesting where the roof is exposed. I wonder what stories are known of this place? Who used to go? Has it seen better days? Do the boarded up windows hide a dark empty space? What

(CHORUS) lies behind the door? The memories of before. 2. Well, it

1.
By the Boathouse on Chesterton Road there's a building
It's all painted white and surrounded by hoardings
For several years now the whole place has been closed
And the birds have been nesting where the roof is exposed
I wonder what stories are known of this place?
Who used to go? Has it seen better days?
Do the boarded up windows hide a dark empty space?
What lies behind the door? The memories of before

2.
Well, it started its life as the Tivoli Cinema
Built in the twenties, Art Deco exterior
An orchestra played for the stars on the screen
All the staff dressed in brown and they kept the place clean
Pay more for a box or you'd sit in the pit
If the Cam rose, then your feet would get wet
It was closed in the fifties when the tax wasn't met
So pull the curtain down, the doors are closing now

3.
When the Tivoli closed it had several careers
There are not many stories well known from these years
But they say it was used for electrical goods
What a strange choice of stock to keep somewhere that floods
No longer a place where the locals could go
Tea breaks replaced all the matinee shows
With a custard cream biscuit and a brew, I suppose
It's time for clocking out, the doors are closing now

4.
Then the three decades after brought pub after pub
From a warehouse of goods to a bustling hub
When first came The Exchange, only there a few months
But it wasn't too long 'til they restocked the pumps
The Fresher and Firkin with brewery on site
Kath brewed fine ales to the punter's delight
Then The Graduate put gigs on and 'a pound a pint' nights
Well, pour the final round, the doors are closing now

5.
Twenty-ten saw the Tivoli title restored
The food prices and specials were chalked on a board
And it seemed like the business was going to plan
Until one fateful morning a big fire began
The water that once touched the filmgoer's toes
Doused out the flames with the firefighter's hose
But the building was damaged and it had to be closed
So, put the fire out, the doors are closing now

A BATTLE OF PLATES

"Inspired by the 2014 cricket match between St Radegund pub and The Haymaker's Arms in Chesterton, this song has players resembling white dots from above, or in heraldic blazon: silver plates. As the Umpire was Milton legend 'Beard', the stage was set."

Guy went to school in Cambridge and teaches Design Technology in nearby Bishop's Stortford. He has released two solo albums, both recorded in CB4. He fought in the Battle of Plates and was clean bowled for a duck, third ball.

By Guy Dinwiddy

1.

I'll tell you a tale of cricket and ale
and fearsome derring do,
They met on a field, a fetching fair field,
ten and one plates fought two.
With leather and willow, a great peccadillo.
A battle of plates, glory awaits!

2.

The Haymaker's Arms (not just from farms),
cheered by a kangaroo.
The team from the Saint without complaint,
let the first blow fall true.
Two bats and a ball, bails rise and they fall.
A battle of plates, glory awaits!

3.

The plates they were told by a red beard so bold
exactly what to do,
And the beard said who's out, who was in and not out,
and they all agreed and played too.
The Saints, well they made hay, the rest had a fine day.
A battle of plates, glory awaits!

4.

They ended up friends (cricket transcends)
and off to the Arms they flew.
Beers overturned, but we all learned
this wasn't Waterloo.
A battle of plates, this song celebrates.
A battle of plates, glory awaits!

 ARBURY CARNIVAL

In 1977, The Arbury Carnival was started by the community for the community and remains true to its founding idea- it is exuberant, colourful and produces a sea of happy faces. This song captures the joy of the Carnival and celebrates how women, kids and men who had never spoken, became best friends.

By Bob Hines

♩. = 112

(CHORUS)

The Ar-bu-ry Car - ni - val, we wel-come one____ and all, bring-ing it past____ your door the car - ni - val. The Ar-bu-ry Car - ni - val, for for-ty years____ or more, do come a - long,____ en - joy the car - ni - val.

1. To
2. To

(VERSE)

1. ce - le - brate the Queen's Ju - bi - lee, what - ev - er we do we want to in - clude the whole com - mu - ni - ty. What do you want? What shall we plan? We ain't done this be - fore, and then it popped out some - one's head: "Let's
2. Camp-kin Road came one, two and three, it start - ed off small but soon it in-volved the whole com - mu - ni - ty. What do we do? What do we wear? I hope you will be there, come join in with us lo - cal folk and

 ARBURY COURT

This song is about a hidden thriving corner in Arbury, bustling with interesting characters and independent shops. It is inspired by Daniel Nestlerode's instrumental 'Humphrey's Waltz' which reflects on living in Humphrey's Road. When writing the lyrics, Caroline interviewed local people for inspiration.

Caroline grew up in CB4, attended local schools including Chesterton Community College, and lives in Arbury. Daniel is a folk musician from Pennsylvania, who lived in Arbury from 2012 to 2018 and recalls; "I will never forget our house, the school where my wife taught, the church I passed walking to Arbury Court, and most of all our lovely and culturally diverse neighbours". Daniel currently resides in France.

By Bob Hines,
Caroline Mead
and Daniel Nestlerode

1. It's hidden away now, on Arbury Road, where the pub's now a Sikh Temple, There are beautiful flowers, shops of all sorts, it's got everything, and it's called Arbury Court. If you're hungry go to Art of Meat, they invented a sausage, a Valentine's treat, For fruit and for veg, spice, pulses and flowers, Les Ward the greengrocer guarantees a smile.

2. Dorringtons Bakers make lovely cake, and it's all nice and fresh, home-made, Tim goes in there daily, 8 on the dot, it's got everything, and it's called Arbury Court. Laura says it's the people she meets, the community feeling that makes it unique. For Sarah it's great to meet up and chat, Quietly thriving, it's Arbury Court.

 BETH SHALOM

This short round is inspired by The Beth Shalom Reform Synagogue in Auckland Road, which is built on the site of the Yasume Club. This was a place where former soldiers captured and enslaved by the Japanese in WW2 could share their experiences. Yasume is Japanese for 'rest' or break from forced labour. The club wound up in 2008 and was bought by The Beth Shalom Jewish community in 2010.

The round can be performed with voices entering at 2 bar intervals (①②③④) or
4 bar intervals (1234) in Hebrew, Japanese or English.

By Emily Peasgood

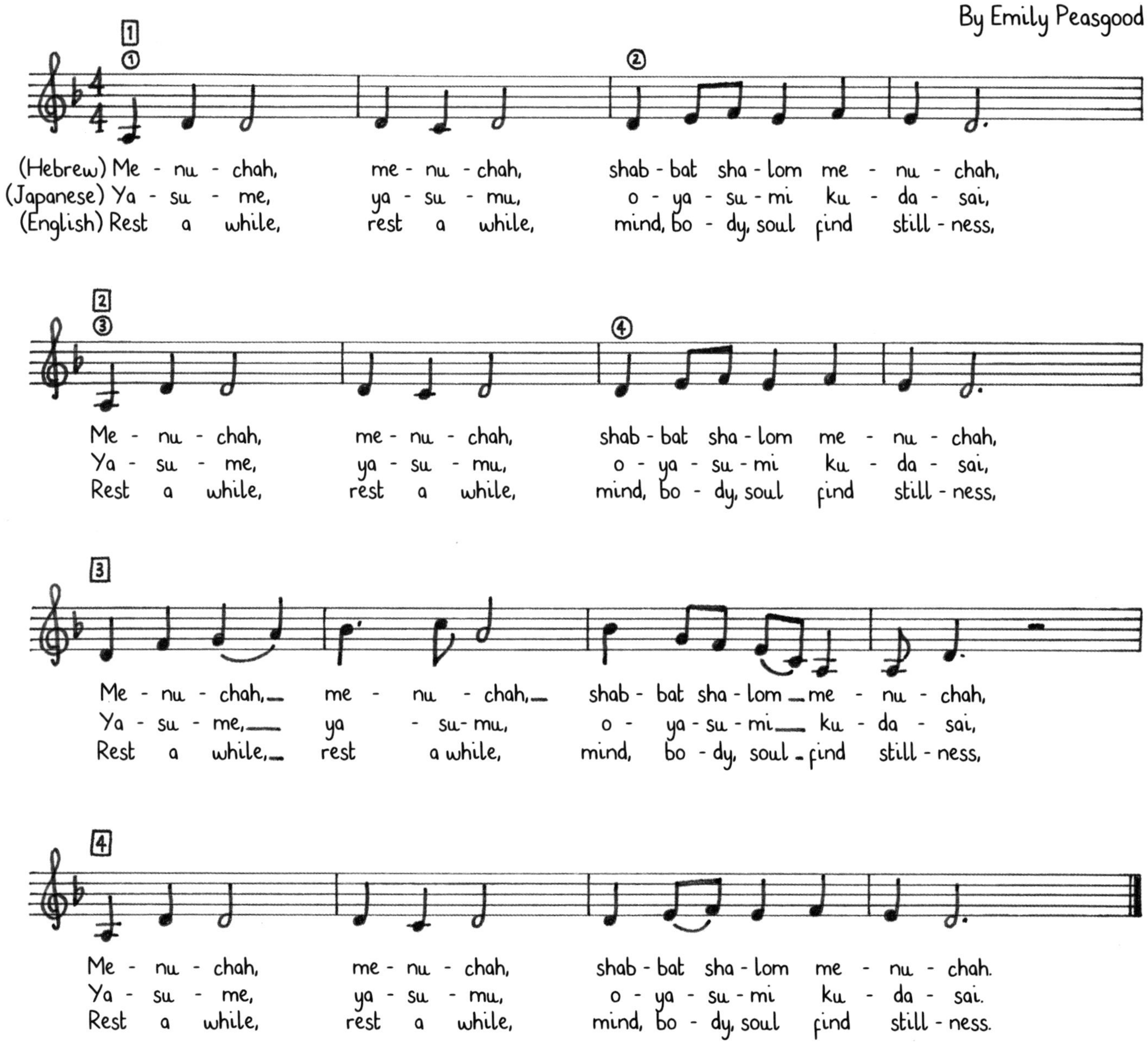

(Hebrew) Me-nu-chah, me-nu-chah, shab-bat sha-lom me-nu-chah,
(Japanese) Ya-su-me, ya-su-mu, o-ya-su-mi ku-da-sai,
(English) Rest a while, rest a while, mind, bo-dy, soul find still-ness,

Me-nu-chah, me-nu-chah, shab-bat sha-lom me-nu-chah,
Ya-su-me, ya-su-mu, o-ya-su-mi ku-da-sai,
Rest a while, rest a while, mind, bo-dy, soul find still-ness,

Me-nu-chah,— me-nu-chah,— shab-bat sha-lom—me-nu-chah,
Ya-su-me,— ya-su-mu, o-ya-su-mi—ku-da-sai,
Rest a while,— rest a while, mind, bo-dy, soul—find still-ness,

Me-nu-chah, me-nu-chah, shab-bat sha-lom me-nu-chah.
Ya-su-me, ya-su-mu, o-ya-su-mi ku-da-sai.
Rest a while, rest a while, mind, bo-dy, soul find still-ness.

LANGUAGE GUIDE

Japanese

Yasume, Yasumu, oyasumi kudasai
休め、休む、お休み下さい。

English translation: Rest, rest, could you please have a rest

Pronunciation guide for English speakers, as written:
Ya-sue-meh, ya-sue-moo, oh-ya-sue-me-coo-da-sigh

Hebrew

Menuchah, menuchah, shabbat shalom menuchah
מְנוּחָה מְנוּחָה שַׁבָּת שָׁלוֹם מְנוּחָה

English Translation: Rest, rest, peaceful sabbath of rest

Pronunciation guide for English speakers, as written and with emphasis on the last syllable of each word:
Men-oo-*chah, men-oo-chah, sha-bat shal-om, men-oo-chah

*ch is pronounced in a similar way to the 'ch' in Loch. There is no official transliteration of this sound in Hebrew. As it is best heard, please seek the advice of a Hebrew speaker and listen to how it is pronounced.

BIG ISSUE

This song is inspired by a Big Issue seller who sleeps in Kings Hedges. Every day, he travels into Cambridge to his pitch outside M&S. This song discusses some of the problems he experienced during lockdown in the spring of 2020.

By Bob Hines
and Emily Peasgood

1. I catch the bus about half past eight, into Cambridge from Downham's Lane, to my place of work, I'm never late, but I'm my own boss, so who's to say? I make some money with the Big Issue, it gives me something good to do, and ev'ry morning, ev'ry afternoon, you'll see life from a different point of view. Doo doo doo doo doo doo doo, doo doo doo ba doo doo doo. Doo doo doo doo doo doo doo doo doodle-oo doo doo doo.

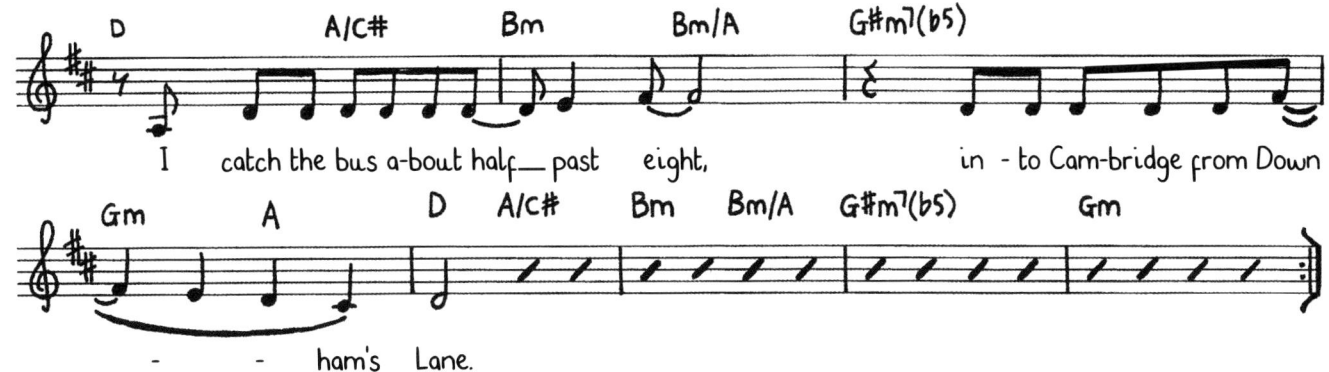

1.
I catch the bus about half past 8, into Cambridge from Downham's Lane
To my place of work, I'm never late, but I'm my own boss, so who's to say?
I make some money with the Big Issue, it gives me something good to do
And ev'ry morning, ev'ry afternoon
You'll see life from a different point of view

2.
And there are those that will turn away, they don't know what I hear them say:
"He's a scally, he is on the make, and he ain't homeless, he's just a fake"
But there are others who will stop and say: "Hello", and pass the time of day
A cup of coffee and a piece of cake
The kind that mmm my momma made

3.
When everybody was safe at home, I was lost with nowhere to go
So, I wound up feeling more alone, some days I felt like the only one
It seemed to me the world had gone to sleep, it brought a familiar kind of peace
But when you live on these deserted streets
Then Wintercomfort is the place you seek

4.
And now that it has all been relaxed, I've finally got my punters back
It feels strange to see the world go by, I can't quite figure the reason why
I guess I missed them more than they missed me, and that's how it will always be
Can't put my finger on what has changed
Some things have gone and some have remained

I catch the bus about half past 8, into Cambridge from Downham's lane

BLACK FEN CLUB BLUES

This song started life as a poem, inspired by a serendipitous duet between a guitarist and a blackbird one warm April evening at the Black Fen Folk Club on Holland Street. Anna is a local writer and folk-fan who composed her first-ever folk song whilst driving to Tesco during lockdown.

By Anna Shelton

(VERSE 1)

Grey-haired gui-tar-ist in sen-si-ble brown shoes, tapped a-way the rhy-thm of his Black Fen Club blues, His fin-gers fret-ted sul-len strings as he sang of black-ened bones, while out-side a black-bird sings in har-mo-ni-sing tones. Oh it's

(CHORUS)

Sun-day night at Folk Club, we come to hear mu-si-cians play, When life is hard their me-lo-dies tran-sport us far a-way, It's a to-nic for the bad times, lifts us high when we are low, Hands clap-ping, feet tap-ping on the stick-y floor, When the mu-sic stops we all cry: "Play one more! Play one more! Play one more! Some-one

(VERSE 2)

squeez-es a me-lo-de-on be-side the red-haired girl, She sweet-ly sings of death and duels, the tales be-gin to twirl. With their bal-lads, reels and shan-ties they will teach us a tune and all our voic-es fill the room, this dar - kened room. Oh it's

REPEAT CHORUS

(VERSE 3) Please ex-cuse the compere with his baw-dy romp so blue. Ig - nore the white-haired heck-ler, he's had a drink or two, But bring out a banjo and my heart o-ver flows, Sing me songs of bow head-ed bar-ley, and fate-ful Bri - ar Rose. Oh it's

REPEAT CHORUS

(VERSE 4) There is-n't much di-ver-si-ty, av-erage age is fif-ty four, and you'll need to play more loud-ly than the creak-ing toil-et door, But a tin flute and a dul-ci-mer beat an orch-es-tra hands down, In the back room of the so-cial club in the north of Cam-bridge town. Oh it's

TO FINAL CHORUS

Final Chorus

(Oh, it's) Sunday night at Folk Club, we come to hear musicians play

When life is hard their melodies transport us far away

We return again each weekend, like the tide runs to the shore

Hands clapping, feet tapping on the sticky floor

When the music stops we all cry: "Play one more! Play one more!"

"Play _____ one more!"

BOATHOUSE

This song laments and celebrates Wednesday evenings at the Boathouse Pub, where lovers of live music from all quarters converged to enjoy the cream of Cambridge musicians. The diamonds added glamour and glitter to create an atmosphere of fun, vibrancy and inclusion. Composer Bob remembers playing there and lyricist Neil was a regular.

Neil is a Foster Carer and songwriter living in Willingham, Cambridge.

By Neil Banks and Bob Hines

(VERSE)
Guitar: palm mute on the beat

Mandolin

1. Ev-'ry Wed-nesday eve-nin' at the Boat-house, I'm peo-ple watch-ing as they come in and out, live mu-sic is what it's all a-bout, let me wel-come you in. It ne-ver mat-tered if it was cold out-side, or you were look-ing for a bet-ter place to hide, it on-ly mat-ters what is

2. Jon-no sang the blues with true e-mo-tion, in his suit of speck-led matte e-mul-sion, and Fred-die sang: 'Stand By Me', we were so troub-le free. We hitched a ride in-to the Del-ta blues and we Walked On Sun-shine wear-ing Blue Suede Shoes and be-side the danc-ers

3. Le-o lived like Ein-stein, re-la-tive-ly, and his el-bow patch-es ne-ver left me, and cou-ples who dis-guised their ro-mance danced the Moon-dance all night. How we miss that lit-tle spin-ning la-dy, and how our Del-la flirt-ed, ve-ry sha-dy, he was she, or she was

1.
Ev'ry Wednesday evenin' at the Boathouse
I'm people watching as they come in and out
Live music is what it's all about
Let me welcome you in
It never mattered if it was cold outside
Or you were looking for a better place to hide
It only matters what is on the inside
Let me welcome you in

Chorus
And the house band drove all night
At the wheel was Johnny Wright
And the Diamond Girls wore diamonds
Red lips and high heel shoes / On their souls and their shoes
Ev'ry Wednesday evenin' at the Boathouse, ooh

2.
Jono sang the blues with true emotion
In his suit of speckled matte emulsion
And Freddie sang: 'Stand By Me'
We were so trouble free
We hitched a ride into the Delta blues and
We Walked On Sunshine wearing Blue Suede Shoes and
Beside our dancers who were on the Wilder Side
We watched worlds collide

Chorus

3.
Leo lived like Einstein, relatively
And his elbow patches never left me
And couples who disguised their romance
Danced the Moondance all night
How we miss that little spinning lady
And how our Della flirted, very shady
He was she, or she was he, well maybe
Everybody come in
Ev'ry Wednesday evenin' at the Boathouse, ooh

4.
The River Cam it keeps on flowing
Skirting CB4 and never slowing
All its pleasures it keeps bestowing
The twists, the turns, the ebbs and flowings
And sat beside the Boathouse just the same
The Wednesday session folded as its hall of fame
Drew the gems that sparkled like a crown
Now sadly taken from this town
But still I hear the sounds of
Ev'ry Wednesday evenin' at the Boathouse (x4)

BURIAL NO. 4

Burial No.4 is widely known as 'The Arbury Skeleton' on display in the museum of Archaeology and Anthropology in Cambridge. It was found in summer 1952 when work on the new Arbury housing estate was taking place, alongside other burials from the late 3rd or 4th century. This song is inspired by the remains of a woman found in 'Burial No.4' and what we know about her: she was a Roman woman in her 40s to early 50s and her burial in a stone lead-lined coffin suggests considerable wealth. We imagine her life as it might have been. This song comprises a verse and a chorus with varied performance options to be interpreted by the performer. An example of how it might be interpreted is provided on the final page.

Lara is a local songwriter who is rediscovering writing. She works at the University of Cambridge.

By Emily Peasgood
and Lara Gisborne

1. My cream is made in Rome, though I know what matters is love and home, I
2. I've lived four score and more, my husband beside laying down the law, We
3. Camilla is my name, contented I am with my modest fame. We'll
4. To see me, woman, dead, I rest a while in my museum bed. And

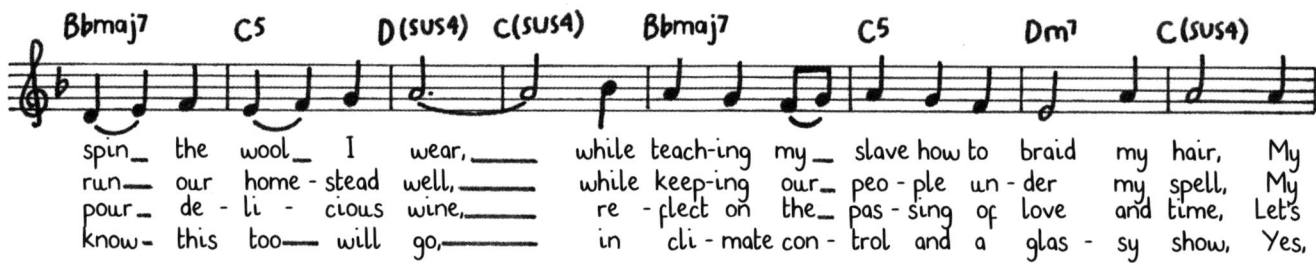

spin the wool I wear, while teaching my slave how to braid my hair, My
run our homestead well, while keeping our people under my spell, My
pour delicious wine, reflect on the passing of love and time, Let's
know this too will go, in climate control and a glassy show, Yes,

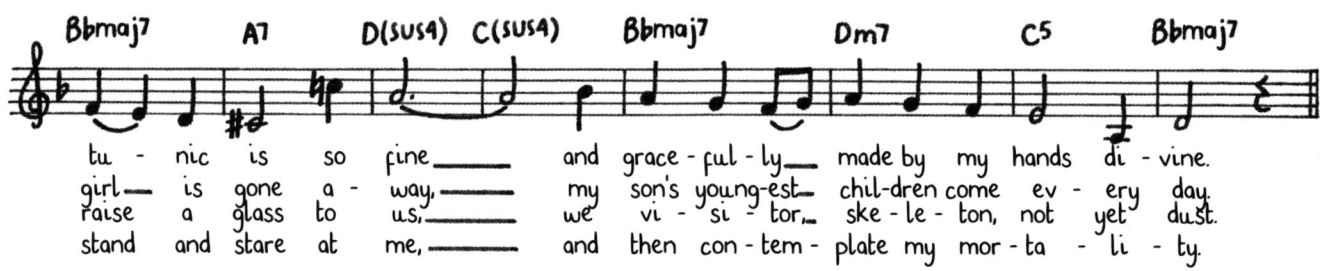

tunic is so fine and gracefully made by my hands divine.
girl is gone away, my son's youngest children come every day.
raise a glass to us, we visitor, skeleton, not yet dust.
stand and stare at me, and then contemplate my mortality.

The verse can be performed as a 3-part round, hummed or with lyrics, with voices entering at 2 bar intervals (①②③) or 4 bar intervals (1 2 3). It can be performed a cappella or with optional instrumentation.

The chorus has a cross-rhythm feel, with optional backing vocals, keyboard (marimba or bone like sound), bass and triangle. Shakers on 16ths and other percussion instruments or samples of TV static can be added at the performers discretion.

INTERPRETATION EXAMPLE

Intro
(Hum the verse as an a cappella round with 3 voices at 2-bar intervals)

1.
(Solo singer, a capella)

My cream is made in Rome, though I know what matters is love and home
I spin the wool I wear, while teaching my slave how to braid my hair
My tunic is so fine and gracefully made by my hands divine.

2.
(Solo singer with piano and bass)

I've lived four score and more, my husband beside laying down the law
We run our homestead well, while keeping our people under my spell
My girl is gone away, my son's youngest children come every day.

Chorus
(Solo singer with backing vocals, keyboard-marimba tone, bass and shaker on 16ths)

Burial Number Four, will I find skeletons at my door? Will I mind?
T.V. comes to life, well I'm kind of worried.
Burial Number Four, status quo, people knock on my door, do they know?
History repeats, and I'm feeling flurried.

3.
(Solo singer with piano and bass)

Camilla is my name, contented I am with my modest fame
We'll pour delicious wine, reflect on the passing of love and time
Let's raise a glass to us, we visitor, skeleton, not yet dust.

Repeat Chorus
(Solo singer with BV's, keyboard-marimba tone, bass, shaker 16ths and triangle)

4.
(Solo singer with piano and bass)

To see me, woman, dead, I rest a while in my museum bed
And know this too will go, in climate control and a glassy show
Yes, stand and stare at me, and then contemplate my mortality.

Repeat Chorus
(Solo singer with BV's, keyboard-marimba tone, bass, shaker 16ths and triangle)

Chorus & V1
(Solo singer with BV's, bass and shaker with simultaneous V1 round: 3 voices at 2-bar intervals)

Ending
(Hum the verse as an a cappella round with 3 voices at 2-bar intervals)

CAMBRIDGE COMMUNITY ARTS

Cambridge Community Arts offer inclusive courses for people to explore their creativity. This song is inspired by Maira's experience of taking part in their music courses, and how it helped her re-centre after moving back to the UK from working as a missionary in Thailand and Asia. It is best accompanied with guitar, percussion and 2-3 backing singers.

Maira is an Irish Australian who lives in Cambridge, having grandparents who hail from Wales and Yorkshire. She enjoys writing poetry and songs, making beats, developing skills in musicianship and working on her home recording studio.

By Maira Kay and Emily Peasgood

(VERSE)

1. When life is hard and I'm in a strange place where I don't even wanna see my face, I don't, I don't know what I'm doing. And sometimes I can't see the wood for the trees. I even struggle looking at the birds and bees, and I don't, I don't know what I'm saying.

2. pitch up when I'm less than my best, I find my heart or get it off my chest when I don't, I don't know what I'm feeling. And sometimes I'm troubled and caught in a bubble, needing to unwind a confusing muddle, I don't, I don't know what I'm thinking.

(CHORUS)

1. Cambridge Community Arts saved me, and I became who I want to be, Now I know, I really know what I'm

2. Cambridge Community Arts saved me, I'm in a world of discovery, Now I know, I really know what I'm

(VERSE 1 + CHORUS 1)
Perform at the same time with two singers. Use minimal guitar for the first 8 bars (breakdown) then fuller guitar with optional backing vocals. BVs can be introduced one harmony at a time.

(VERSE 2 + CHORUS 2)
Perform at the same time with two singers. Continue with fuller guitar for the first 8 bars then cut guitar out for the final 8. Optional backing vocals can continue unaccompanied to end.

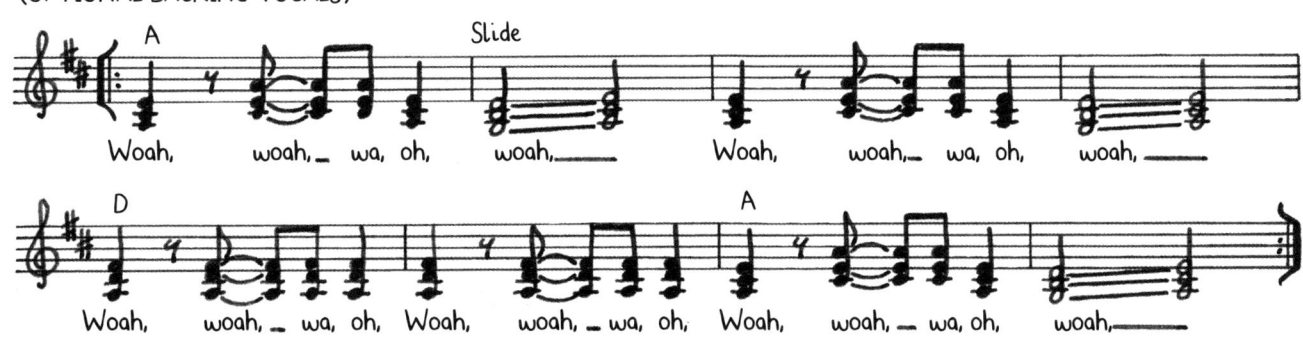

CHESTERTON ALLOTMENT SOCIETY

"My allotment has brought me a lot of joy and feeds my family healthy food which tastes so much better than the shop bought veggies. It's close to home but feels like a journey into the country. There is a pond for frogs to breed and eat the slugs and my family often visit to help out and have a picnic."

Liz is a granny who enjoys singing, plays flute, accordian and Indian harmonium and takes part in orchestras and folk clubs in Cambridge. She was born in Australia and lived in India before settling in Chesterton in the 70s.

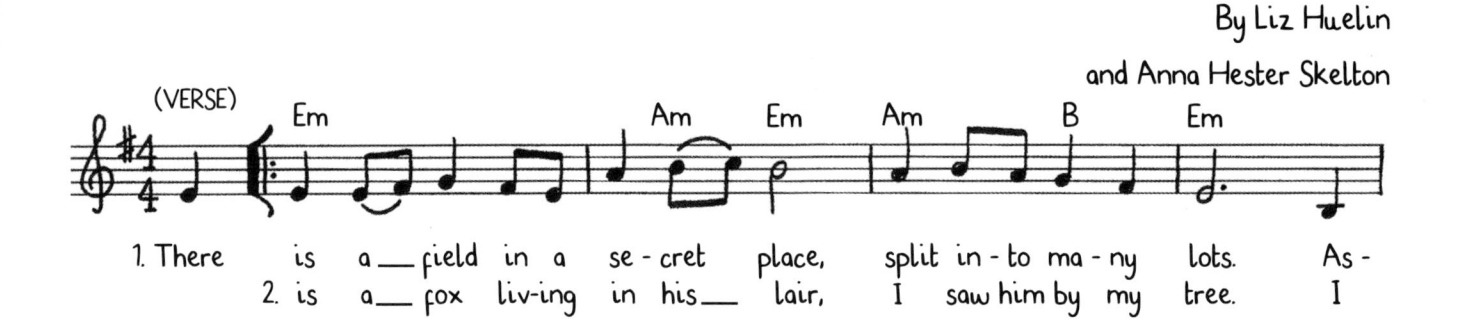

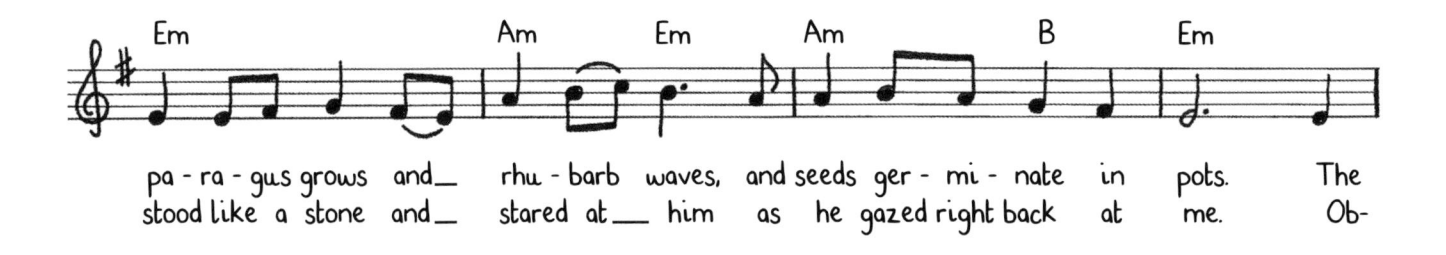

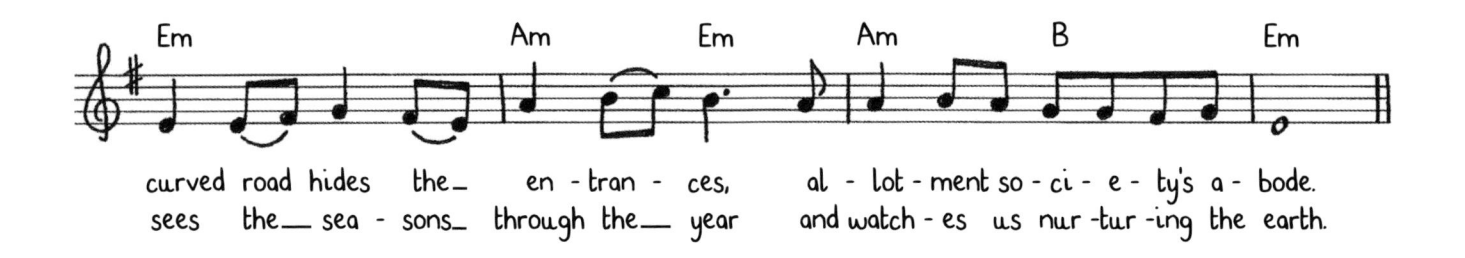

By Liz Huelin
and Anna Hester Skelton

1. There is a field in a secret place, split into many lots. Asparagus grows and rhubarb waves, and seeds germinate in pots. The road goes off from Union Lane, the gates hidden from the road. Its curved road hides the entrances, allotment society's abode.

2. is a fox living in his lair, I saw him by my tree. I stood like a stone and stared at him as he gazed right back at me. Observing from two streets away: the tower of St Georges Church. It sees the seasons through the year and watches us nurturing the earth.

(CHORUS)

Who'll come a-long with us to-day, armed with a fork and a rake?

Come and pick the straw-ber-ries, put seeds in the beds we make.

2. There make.

1.

There is a field in a secret place, split into many lots.

Asparagus grows and rhubarb waves, and seeds germinate in pots.

The road goes off from Union Lane, the gates hidden from the road.

Its curved road hides the entrances, Allotment Society's abode.

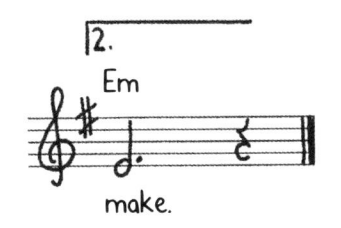

Chorus

Who'll come along with us today, armed with a fork and a rake?

Come and pick the strawberries, put seeds in the beds we make.

2.

There is a fox living in his lair, I saw him by my tree.

I stood like a stone and stared at him as he gazed right back at me.

Observing from two streets away: the tower of St Georges Church.

It sees the seasons through the year and watches us nurturing the earth.

Chorus

CHESTERTON WALTZ

"Chesterton Waltz is inspired by three of my favourite places: the spacious and peaceful Old Chesterton Allotments, the historic Green Dragon pub and the Haymakers, with its rich tradition of music making. These fiddle tunes form a trio that reflects the history, character and community spirit of each place and of Chesterton itself."

Sharon is a local violinist, composer and teacher, often seen cycling around with a violin on her back.

♩=152 Lively Waltz

Pakenham Close

By Sharon Sullivan

At the end of Pakenham Close there's the Old Chesterton Allotment Society site. It's a peaceful haven; an escape from the busyness and stress of modern life. All sorts of people grow veg, fruit and flowers on their plots, amongst the insects and birds, and foxes and frogs.

The Merry Haymakers

This pub has a long history of music and dancing, from World War 2 era sing-alongs to blues jams and cover bands. It is better known today for its large selection of real ales and excellent pizza, but if you're lucky you can still catch a band now and again.

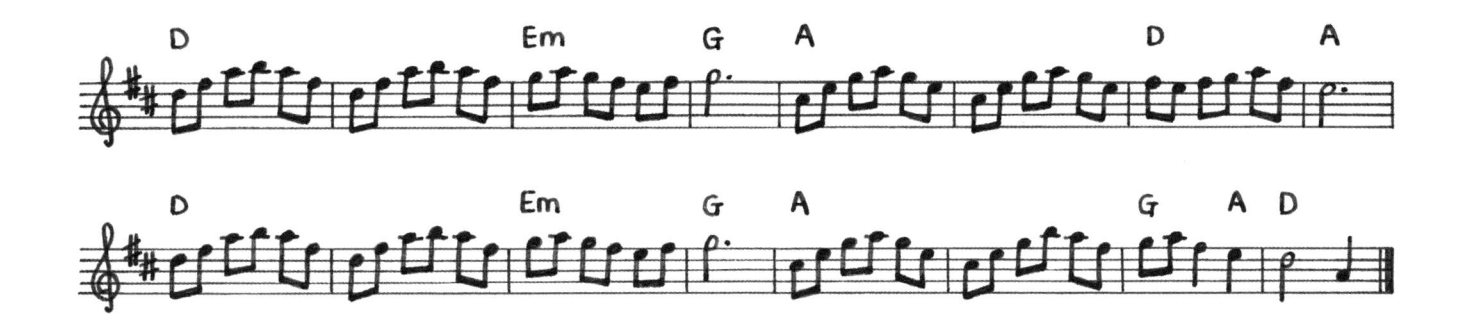

Green Dragon on the Cam / The Missing Ferryman

This lovely pub with its garden by the river has been part of community life for hundreds of years. Frequented by Oliver Cromwell and J.R.R. Tolkien, the place is steeped in history. Mystery was added when a local ferryman disappeared after leaving the pub one evening.

DATING IN CB4

This song is inspired by Eleana's dating experiences in CB4. There are two chorus options to choose from. Option 1 requires omitting the last word of verses 2 and 3. Verse 4 ends abruptly on "boo". This song is sung, and spoken in parts with improvised ad libs to describe frustrating dating experiences.

Eleana grew up in Arbury, is a keen amateur photographer and studies Performing Arts at Anglia Ruskin University.

By Eleana Ray
and Emily Peasgood

Laid Back Funky Guitar ♩ = 120

(VERSE)

1. First time I met Ronnie, we went to the Golden Hind, he said: "Do you like gaming?" - I said: "I don't mind". He told me 'bout the planets and looking at the stars, I
2. First time I met Tommy, we went to The Waterman, he asked me for a cuddle, I said: "No, no thanks!" He said: "I am a model, and have great angles too", I
3. First time I met Jonny, we went to the Milton Arms, he said: "I think you're lovely", he was full of charm. He told me all the cute girls have lots of attitude, I
4. First time I met Robbie, we walked by the river Cam, he said: "I really like you, I'm your biggest fan". He talked about his spreadsheets, how not to overspend, I

Fmaj7 / **G**

rolled my eyes and said: "Is there life on Mars?"
slumped in-to the chair, but he was-n't through, he said:
said: "O-kay, that's nice. Shall we or-der food?"—
freaked out when he said: "Are we more than friends?"

Am7 / **C**

"Wan-na play Nin-ten-do? We can play Star Wars,
"I don't go on bus-es, I think I'm real cool,
"I can or-der for you, I am a good guy,
"You can come to my place, but pre-tend we're mates,

Fmaj7 / **G**

you be Princ-ess Lei-a, I will be The Force."
I work at a jewel-ler and I have a pool".
how a-bout fa-ji-tas then some ap-ple pie?"
if we see my lod-ger, we're not on a date."

Am7 / **C**

I don't know what I want or what I'm look-ing for, I
I don't know if I want to see these guys a-gain, I
I don't know if I want a guy who thinks he's boss, I
I knew I did-n't want a guy with-out a clue, I

Fmaj7

wish I knew the ans-wer, Ron-nie was a
wish I knew the ans-wer, Tom-my was too
wish I knew the ans-wer, Jon-ny made me
think I found the ans-wer: I don't need a--->(To END Page 45)

(Guitar back in) (Vamp during ad libs, then return to verse)

|1. **Am7** / **Fmaj7** / **G**

bore. (Spoken ad lib about the frustrations of dating...)

43

(CHORUS OPTION 1)

|2. 3.

Am / **F**
Da-ting in North Cam-bridge, are these guys for real?

Am / **G**
Fine wine, love and di-ning, had a nice ap-peal. I say:

Am / **F**
"Night, night, see you la-ter". They say: "Good-night beau-ti-ful". But

Eb / **Bb** / **G7** (Unaccompanied)
then they go and ruin it by say-ing: (Spoken cheesy chat up line, into ad libs

Am7 / **FMaj7** / **G** (TO VERSE Page 42)
about the frustrations of dating...)

(CHORUS OPTION 2)

|2.3.|

2. vain. He was a bor-ing, bor-ing bon-ny boy-o,
3. cross He was a bos-sy, bos-sy bon-ny boy-o,

he was a bon - ny, bor - ing boy.
he was a bon - ny, bos - sy boy.

He was a bor - ing, bor - ing bon-ny boy-o,
He was a bos - sy, bos - sy bon-ny boy-o,

(To VERSE Page 42)

he was a bon - ny, bor - ing boy.
he was a bon - ny, bos - sy boy.

(END)

4. boo.

ELIZA

In 1799, Impington resident Elizabeth Woodcock was buried in the snow for eight days. She survived the horrendous ordeal, but never truly recovered and died six months later. This song captures how her husband Daniel must have felt; frantic with worry, and devastated when she did not recover. Daniel died shortly after Eliza, leaving their son William orphaned.

By Guy Dinwiddy

(VERSE 1)

Some called her E-li-za-beth, but I called her Eliza, we'd been mar-ried three years gone, then I lost her, I lost her in the snow. We walked out of our church, to have and to hold, Did she re-mem-ber that as her feet grew cold? Ice went

(CHORUS)

in-to her heart, in-to her veins, E-li-za, where have you gone? I've called and tried and cried.

Alternative lyric: She ne-ver thawed out my love left and tore my world a-part.

(VERSES 2-5)

2. She went ri-ding through the snow on a horse that she called Tin-ker, Flash! And Tin-ker reared up so high, and she lost him, she lost him in the snow.

1.
I have lived on Fen Road for more than twenty-five years
We are deeply ashamed of what's happening
It's the fault of some youngsters; young men in their prime
And their actions, they know what they're doing

2.
When I go to the shops I must apologise
They don't see I'm a man of good standing
We are just as frustrated as others, you see
And we don't all deserve this harsh branding

3.
One bad apple can taint the whole barrel, it's true
And we're all just as bad as each other, they say
But we can't bear the blame for what we didn't do
And a man's not an apple to be thrown away

4.
On 'The Wild West' Fen Road, as it has come to be known
Where the actions of some bring us shaming
We have tried to escape all the stigma we face
But to many we're always for blaming

5.
I'm a man of few words but I will take it on board
By and large it's the only way to it
When we all bear the shame of a few who're to blame
Quiet grace is the only way through it

6.
Now then it doesn't matter where you're going, it's true
'Cause it's always who you have beside you
But if cold-faced disdain is on each face you meet
Then you'll wish the ground open and hide you

Chorus
A few bad apples
A few bad apples

G.O.A.T.

"LL Cool J fans and all Hip Hop heads know G.O.A.T stands for Greatest Of All Time. This is a few words of warning to parents searching for the one birthday present that will make their 13 year old smile."

Lucille is a writer and choreographer, a product of north of the river, long-term-full-time Arburynaut and a third of the creative drive behind world famous Arts and Culture organisation, SIN Cru.

By Lucille Rococoa

I've   loved other guys.
I've   looked into their eyes
but this was supposed to be no strings
now wethered, you're tethered
by some reinforced acrylic to a tree
surrounded by mud, carrot ends and

We fetched you from a council estate
outside 'boro
Just you, me in the car, and my daughter.
Her smile was unusually constant and Cheshire.
You calmed the sulky understudy of a woman and let her
love you.

Last night we left you on a temporary bed
of fresh   wood shavings.
You escaped from the first
squeezing your balls through the cattle stalls
and were moved to the stable block
where you could be   locked in.

I've   heard all the lines
I've   cried (o) so many times
but when the peelers came round
on Boxing Day morning,
I knew you was wandering.
I could guess what was coming

Pulled my dressing gown
down over the bruise on my thigh
never as high as the ribs you can't reach
and for a moment, I enjoyed the silence.
No head butting walls and braying
It's hard to explain you're only play

In the court a crowd had gathered
fencing you in,
preventing you from
entering through the
automatic supermarket
doors.   But stubborn, you weren't Budgens.

Now a full page spread in the local news,
exaggerated views from readers,
reports from the pub cleaners
who were chased down the road
and had to hide in a bush
but you's keeping stush - no comment, it read.

I've   fell for other smiles
I've   walked a thousand miles
but no matter where I go
I unintentionally smell of you
No Paco Rabanne, Lynx, or even Magic Tree
your front legs, chest, face, and beard are all covered in

We were advised it was a wise procedure
and raised £80 to debase you.
I always thought your sack
hung like Bajan soursops
protected by Emerald City carrier bags to stop
the monkeys from pinching them.

Teeth sunk softly into a squidgey
dumpling made from glutinous rice.
Sticky lips rimmed with all things nice -
wrong choice of snack for that day
as the red bean and millet jelly
reminded me only of your operation.

A lack of loyalty unfortunately's not new to me
so I knew as you've reached puberty
you were roaming, you cad,
looking for love,
wearing your own musk,
and it was worse during rut.

Maybe now you'll lose your bravado,
no more Arbury psycho.
But my daughter wants to rehome you.
So if you should ever doubt,
wonder what love is all about,
Just think back and remember babes
if you hadn't eaten my knickers, maybe you could have stayed.

Copyright © Lucille Rococoa, 2015

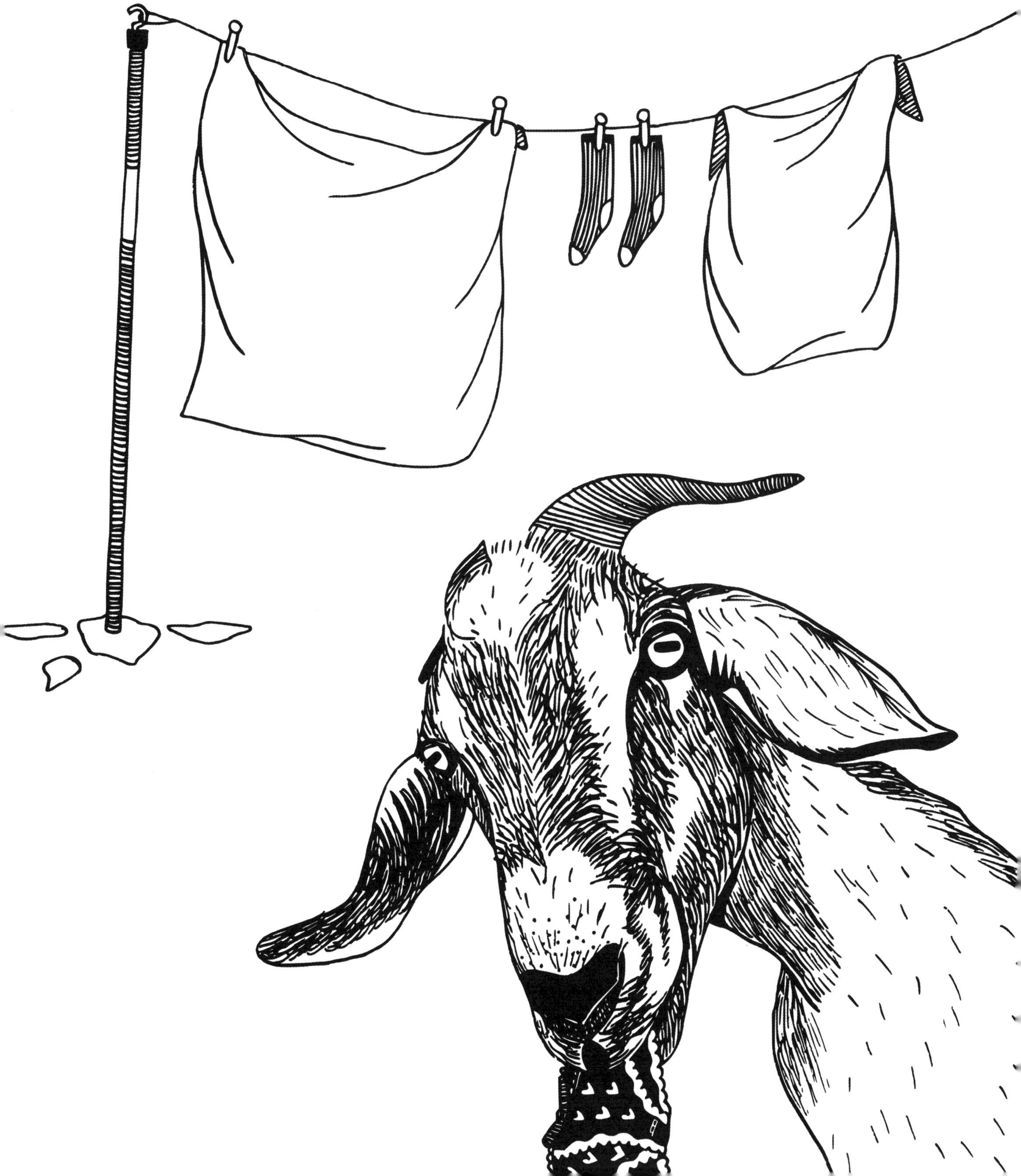

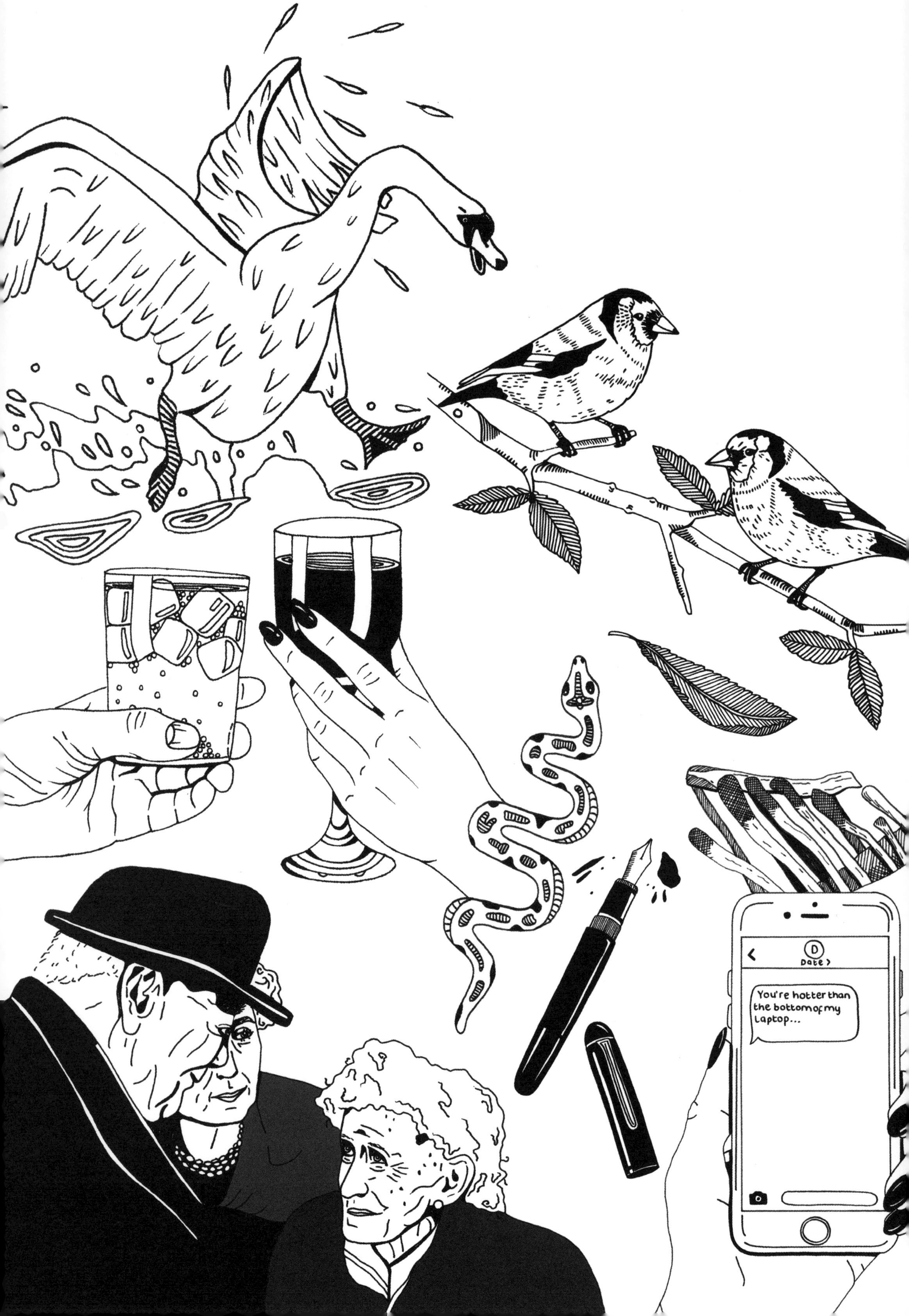
D
Date >
You're hotter than the bottom of my Laptop...

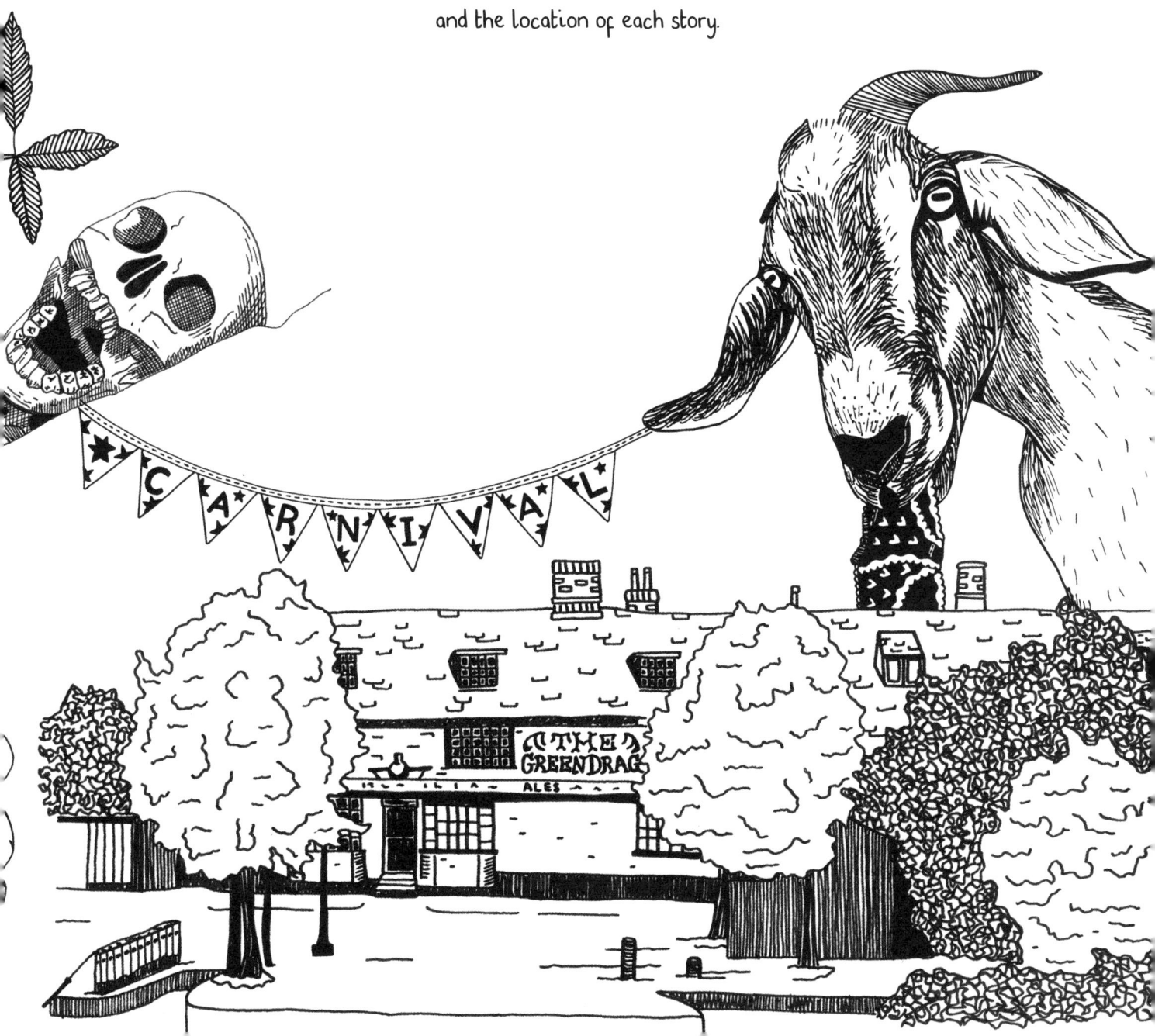

MAP OF SONGS & VERSES

Every song and verse can be mapped to a location or journey in north Cambridge. Specific locations, buildings and landmarks are celebrated in songs like 16 Chesterton Road, Grumpy's Pet Shop and Kindness is Always in Season. Other pieces capture more general locations with an interesting history or a feeling to share, like the histories surrounding Burial No. 4, Halifax Road or Union House, or the sense of community spirit in Arbury Court and Green End Road. Some songs and verses reference several locations or capture a specific journey. The famous herons in Heron Man can be seen in two locations, and we can observe the route the Arbury Carnival procession takes, the Big Issue seller's daily walk to his pitch outside M&S, and the rave convoy that travelled around the city in The Summer of 1989 and collected people from Milton Tescos. This map locates each song in its specific place. Please use it to find stories at specific locations, and the location of each story.

MAP OF SONGS & VERSES

PAGE NO. & KEY

- 14   16 CHESTERTON ROAD
- 16   A BATTLE OF PLATES
- 18   ARBURY CARNIVAL
- 20   ARBURY COURT
- 22   BETH SHALOM
- 24   BIG ISSUE
- 26   BLACK FEN CLUB BLUES
- 28   BOATHOUSE
- 32   BURIAL NO.4
- 36   CAMBRIDGE COMMUNITY ARTS
- 38   CHESTERTON ALLOTMENT SOCIETY
- 40   CHESTERTON WALTZ
- 42   DATING IN CB4
- 46   ELIZA
- 48   FEN ROAD
- 50   G.O.A.T.
- 58   GREEN END ROAD
- 60   GRUMPY'S PET SHOP
- 62   HALIFAX ROAD
- 64   HERON MAN
- 66   KINDNESS IS ALWAYS IN SEASON
- 68   NHS CLAP
- 70   RIVER SHANTY
- 72   SEASONS
- 76   STEAMROLLER PARK
- 80   STRAWBERRY FAIR
- 82   THE BALLAD OF MR ASBO
- 86   THE GHOST OF THE SNOWCAT
- 88   THE SHARING SHELF
- 90   THE SUMMER OF 1989
- 92   TURIN THE PYTHON
- 94   UNION HOUSE
- 98   WHEN DAISY MET WINSTON
- 102   WHEN JONNY PLAYS

Map

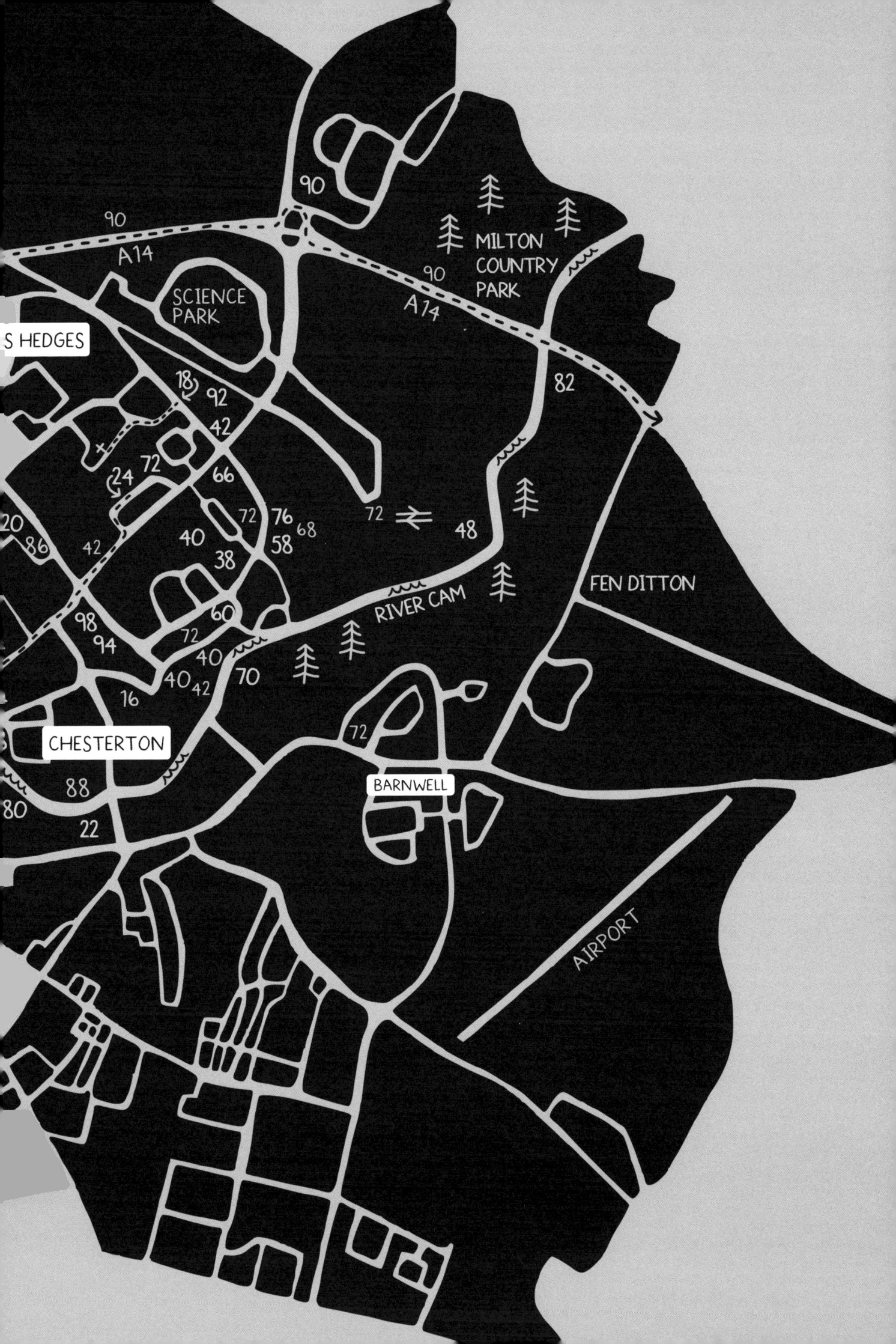

S HEDGES

90
A14

SCIENCE PARK

MILTON COUNTRY PARK

90
A14

82

18 92
42
24 72
66
20 72 76 68
86 42 40 72 58 48
38
98 60
94 72
40 70
40 42
16

FEN DITTON

RIVER CAM

72

CHESTERTON

88
80 22

BARNWELL

AIRPORT

GREEN END ROAD

"I have lived in CB4 since January 2008. I have travelled up and down Green End Rd innumerable times since, and always liked the name. Especially since the 20mph limit was introduced, it has a lovely local feel to it."

George is a professional songwriter and travelling musician.

By George Bacon

♩ = 100

(INTRO)

(VERSE 1) This Cam-bridge street with a pub at one end and a pet store at the oth-er, from Grum-py's to the Gol-den Hind, you can walk or take a bus down

(REFRAIN) Green End Road, an end-less prom-ise, our way in, our way out. Green End Road, a went-way, with C B 4 gath-ered round you.

(VERSE 2) Through the heart of our neigh-bour-hood, where the green and end-ings dwell, at the end of the high street, there it be-gins four bus stops long,

REPEAT REFRAIN

(INSTRUMENTAL) | D | G D | A D | G D | A D

(VERSE 3)
Past the play-ground swings and round - a - bouts, a foot - ball pitch, and sha-dy trees, Mace Off Li - cense, Ches-ter-ton Prim-ary a Meth-o-dist Church, Ni-sa Lo - cal,

(REFRAIN)
Green End Road, an end - less prom-ise, our way in, our way out.

Green End Road, a went way, with C B 4 gath - ered round you.

Green End Road, Green End Road,

Copyright ©
George Bacon, 2020

GRUMPY'S PET SHOP

"I had so much fun writing Grumpy's Pet Shop because it let me express my feelings of love, joy and happiness about animals, and my excitement in visiting Lulu and the nice people at Grumpy's who help me care for my pets, especially my chickens Summer and Poppet."

Chiara is eight years old and attends Chesterton Primary School. Her friends include chickens, dogs, tortoises, moths, guinea pigs, cats, fish and other children. Grumpy's pet shop can be accompanied on piano or guitar.

By Chiara Berry, Genevieve Berry and Emily Peasgood

♩ = 160

(INTRO) Bb

(VERSE) Bb
1. In Ches-ter-ton on Scot-land Road, near the school and church and park,

Bb Eb Cm Eb F7 Bb
You'll find Grum-py's pet shop and when dogs walk by they bark, bark, bark!

Bb
Rich-ard and Ju-lie are there to chat, 'bout your pets n' this n' that. Slide up on 'Oo'
There

(CHORUS) Bb Eb Bb F Bb F
was an old man named Mis-ter Grum-py, and he owned a shop, a pet shop,

Bb F (Clap!) Bb
When he died they named the shop: Mis-ter Grum-py's, Grum-py's pet shop.

(Optional: repeat last two bars)

1.

In Chesterton on Scotland Road, near the school and church and park
You'll find Grumpy's pet shop and when dogs go by they bark, bark, bark!
Richard and Julie are there to chat 'bout your pets n' this n' that
Ooh. . .

Chorus
(Repeat after each verse)
There was an old man named Mister Grumpy
And he owned a shop, a pet shop
When he died they named the shop:
Mister Grumpy's, Grumpy's pet shop

2.

Go see Lulu the cockatoo, when you're there she'll talk to you
She'll shout if you walk away, she really wants to play, play, play!
She talks softly just to kids, and she doesn't have eyelids
Ooh. . .

3.

My cheeky chickens they were blue, lying in the chicken coop
So we took a stroll to Grumpy's and we bought some food, food, food!
Oats and seeds and barley too, now they do nutritious poo
Ooh. . .

4.

My guinea pig was feeling grumpy, 'cause his arms and legs are stumpy
And his brother's bed was lumpy, so we went to Grump, Grump, Grumpy's!
It cheered them up right away, when we gave them straw and hay
Ooh. . .

5.

There's treats for dogs and cats and fish, all can find a tasty dish
Turtles, ferrets, hedgehogs, rabbits, everything you wish, wish, wish!
Monkeys, eels and dolphins too, it's your friendly local zoo!
Ooh. . .

6.

We skip and run and jump and hop, all the way to Grumpy's shop
Near and far and far and wide, please let us come inside, side, side!
People and animals all agree, Grumpy's is the place to be
Ooh. . .

HALIFAX ROAD

"I used to live in a former Victorian almshouse on Halifax Road. This song is inspired by many different lives played out there over the centuries. All the stories mentioned are true."

Jessica is a Cambridge-based singer-songwriter. As well as releasing two studio albums, Jessica used to be a costumed history guide at the Black Country Living Museum.

By Jessica Law
and Anna Hester Skelton

1. I can see the ghosts of those who walked this road in years be-fore,

Har-ry Bra-zier's se-ven chil-dren played be-tween these nar-row walls,

Hid-den dag-gers sparked a scan-dal thir-ty me-tres from my door,

War-time wi-dows paced these ve-ry floors my dan-cing shoes now score. Cross the

street, a ta-vern lies a-sleep; displaced ah_____ Just a

house, the paint-ed name e-rased: blank space, ah_____ And

(CHORUS)

do you see what I see? Do you feel the things I feel? And are you in tune with me? Do you think it might be real? Do you think it might be real? Do you think it might be real?

1.
I can see the ghosts of those who walked this road in years before
Harry Brazier's seven children played between these narrow walls
Hidden daggers sparked a scandal thirty metres from my door
Wartime widows paced these very floors my dancing shoes now score
Cross the street
A tavern lies asleep; displaced (Ah...)
Just a house
The painted name erased: blank space (Ah...)

Chorus
And do you see what I see?
Do you feel the things I feel?
And are you in tune with me?
Do you think it might be real?
Do you think it might be real?
Do you think it might be real?

2.
I can sense what one tree meant to lovers, fighters, thieves and stoats
I can find the signs of lives inscribed in stone or scratched on posts
Metal sparrows guard the park and watch the runners stretch and boast
While the River Cam plays host to different lives on different boats
In these lanes
A history is made each day (Ah...)
On stone stage
We come and go away, it stays (Ah...)

Chorus

HERON MAN

Heron Man is a piece of house music by Darren Fitzpatrick, inspired by the anonymous graffiti artist who paints herons around Cambridge. The rhythms, melodic lines and harmonies created by Darren are presented here as individual parts. Performers are invited to layer, mix and match them in any order for any musical instruments to create their own unique version of Heron Man.

Darren has lived in Cambridge all his life and enjoys creating poetry, music, art, sewing and crafting and has a photography studio.

126bpm

By Darren Fitzpatrick

(SPOKEN WORD - SECTION 1)

I am the he-ron man. I do draw-ings of he-rons a-cross Cam-bridge, I wish to re-main a-non-y-mous, a-non-y-mous.

(SPOKEN WORD - SECTION 2)

In north Cam-bridge they're on Mil-ton Road and Je-sus Lock Bridge. There's prob'bly more, there's some at Tes-co's, have you seen them?

(SPOKEN WORD - SECTION 3)

Heron sounds

He-rons are my fav-'rite birds,

(Heron sounds)

I en-joy watch-ing them in flight,

to see hap-py birds.

(SYNTH MOTIF 1)

(SYNTH MOTIF 2)

(SYNTH MOTIF 3)

(BASS MOTIF 1)

(BASS MOTIF 2)

(PERCUSSION: STANDARD GROOVE)

Hi-hats / shaker

Hand clap

Hand drum

Bass drum

Flexible Instruments

(PERCUSSION: BREAK DOWN / BUILD UP)

Crash cymbal

Flexible Instruments

KINDNESS IS ALWAYS IN SEASON

In August 2017, artists Dan Biggs, Sa'adiah Khan and Samirah Khan created a community mural in Chesterton. It states 'Kindness is Always in Season' and features suggestions from local residents, Brown's Field Youth and Community Centre and Eddie's, a local charity supporting people with learning disabilities. As it was painted passers-by contributed additional ideas. This song captures a few of them.

By Emily Peasgood and Bob Hines

(VERSE)
1. On the corner of Milton and of Green End Road, at a junction where cars hurry by, on the wall of the Co-op is a mural for kindness where you can look and think for a while. If you need a reason why it was done, kindness is always in season.

2. It was

(BRIDGE)
If you love your son, we'll paint for your son. If you want some kindness, we'll give you some. For kindness is always, always in season.

We all need something we can believe in. If...

Refrain x 2, then V1 to finish.

1.
On the corner of Milton and of Green End Road
At a junction where the cars hurry by
On the wall of the Co-op is a mural for kindness
Where you can look and think for a while
If you need a reason why it was done, kindness is always in season

2.
It was painted by Sa'adiah, Samirah and Dan
As a symbol of kindess and peace
They listened to voices of Chesterton people
And painted it all on a Chesterton street
If you need a reason why it was done, kindness is always in season

3.
As they were painting and people passed by
Sa'adiah would look up and say:
"What do you love?" "We love our son;
He died aged eighteen and he's not gone away"
If you need a reason why it was done, kindness is always in season

4.
And they carried on painting, still people came by
They would look up and again:
"What do you love?" "We'd love some kindness,
To brighten up this cold and dark day"
If you need a reason why it was done, kindness is always in season

Bridge
If you love your son, we'll paint for your son
If you want some kindess, we'll give you some
For kindness is always, always in season
We all need something we can believe in
If you need a reason why it was done, kindness is always in season
If you need a reason why it was done, kindness is always in season

Repeat 1.

NHS CLAP

"We created this song to celebrate the sense of community shown by the clap for carers to support hard-working keyworkers during the 2020 lockdown."

Nicola lives in Hardwick, works in Cambridge and is a member of the St Neots Folk Club. Her daughter Chloe is 9 years old and a keen musician, learning recorder and flute.

By Chloe Floyd,
Nicky Floyd
and Bob Hines

(INTRO) (Recorder)

Get out for the N H S clap clap. 1. It

1. start-ed with one on her own, by the next week the num-ber had grown,

ev'ry-one o-pened their doors, a hun-dred, a thou-sand or more.

Lis-ten to the Ar-bury Es-tate, ev'ry Thurs-day eve-ning at 8! A-

(CHORUS)

no-ther week gone and we're back, do-ing the N H S clap. A-

no-ther week gone and we're back, do-ing the N H S clap.

(Recorder) Clap Clap Clap Clap

68

1.
It started just one on her own, by the next week the number had grown
Ev'ryone opened their doors, a hundred, a thousand or more
Listen to the Arbury Estate, ev'ry Thursday evening at 8!

Chorus
Another week gone and we're back, doing the NHS clap
Another week gone and we're back, doing the NHS clap

2.
From the doorsteps along Humphreys Road, to the children who live on The Grove
We clap as much as we can; a small way of giving our thanks
Listen to Kings Hedges Estate, ev'ry Thursday evening at 8!

Chorus

Come on and don't be late, ev'ry Thursday evening at 8!

3.
Bring all your pots and your pans, you should make as much noise as you can
Clapping for carers tonight, our heroes must keep up the fight
Coming out one by one, ev'rybody in Chesterton!

Chorus

RIVER SHANTY

"Living by the Cam is eternally intriguing, inspiring, soothing and rejuvenating. It pumps life through Cambridge joining land and water, flora, fauna and people and it connects us all. This is our shanty for the River: long may it thrive. It takes the form of a traditional call-and-response sea shanty: the first two bars are called by the shanty-person with singers responding. Singers are invited to choose the words for each response, with examples provided in brackets below. The response can be harmonised freely. There are two rhythmic variants with corresponding verses. Have a go at making up some of your own!"

Gen is from Queensland and feels fortunate to be part of Chesterton's warm and welcoming community since 2018.

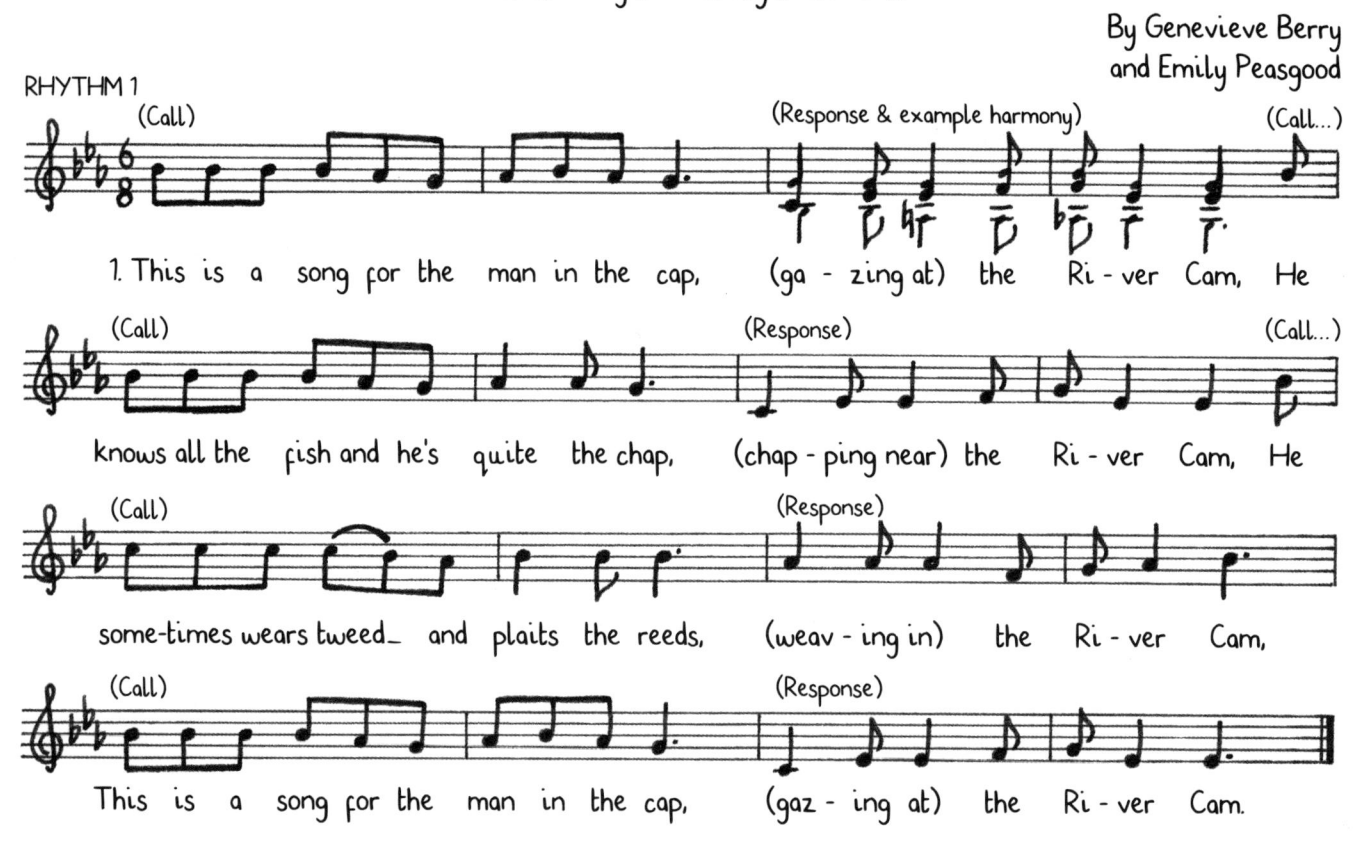

By Genevieve Berry and Emily Peasgood

RHYTHM 1

1. This is a song for the man in the cap, (gazing at) the River Cam, He knows all the fish and he's quite the chap, (chapping near) the River Cam, He sometimes wears tweed and plaits the reeds, (weaving in) the River Cam, This is a song for the man in the cap, (gazing at) the River Cam.

2.
This is a song about Asbo the Swan, (squawking in) the River Cam
He'll chase you away if you do him wrong, (chasing in) the River Cam
He's rather an antisocial bird, (violent in) the River Cam
(Repeat first line)

3.
This is a song for the old Pike and Eel, (burning by) the River Cam
No longer a place for beer and ale, (thirsty by) the River Cam
The old ferry crossing is no more, (cannot cross) the River Cam

4.
This is a song for the Lady De Clare, (haunting by) the River Cam
They say several jealous men murdered her, (murdered by) the River Cam
She's called 'The Black Widow of the Cam', (widowed by) the River Cam

5.
This is a song for what could lie ahead, (future of) the River Cam
Will bicycles line the old water bed? (Cycling in) the River Cam
The river's outflow is very low, (nothing of) the River Cam

RHYTHM 2

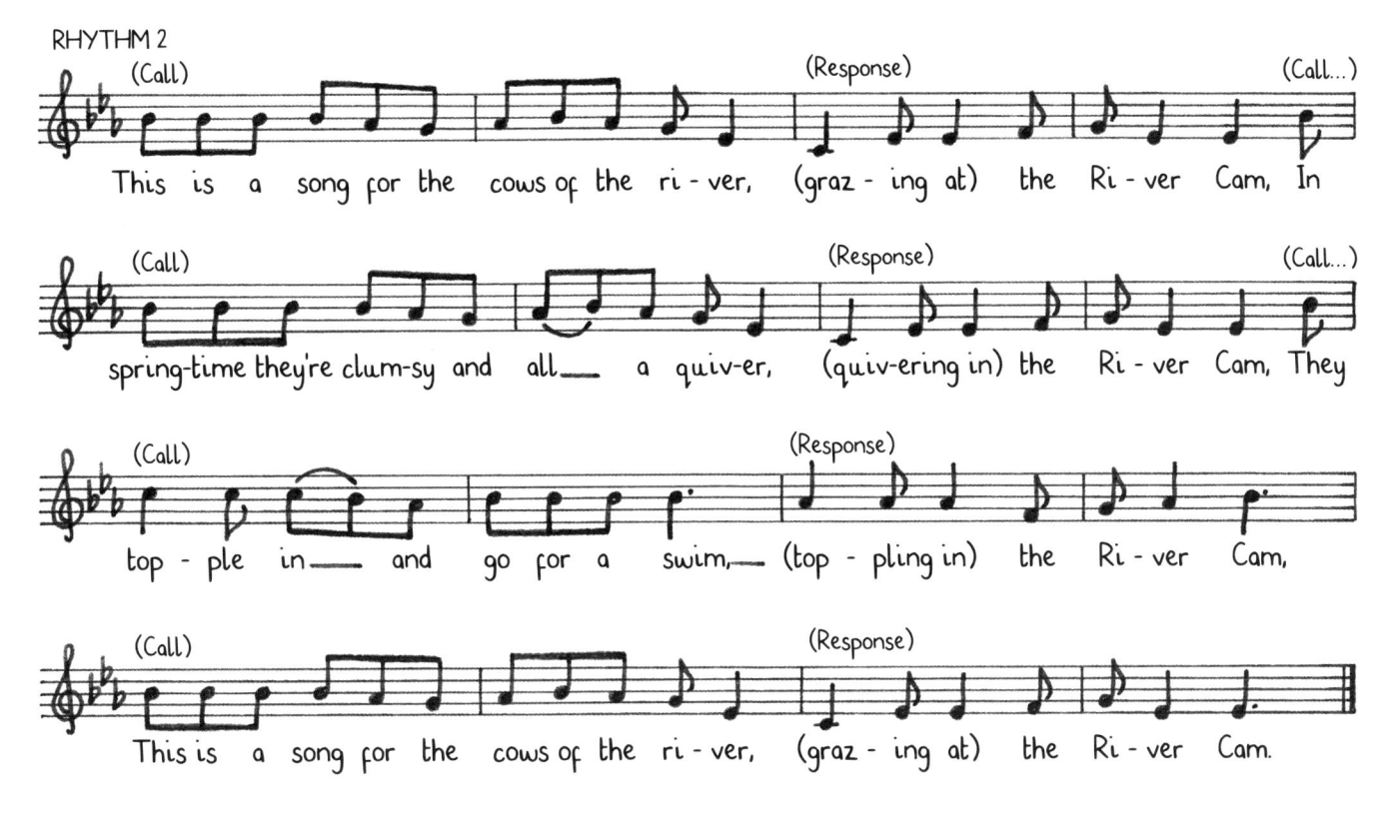

(Call) ... (Response) ... (Call...)
This is a song for the cows of the ri-ver, (graz-ing at) the Ri-ver Cam, In

(Call) ... (Response) ... (Call...)
spring-time they're clum-sy and all a quiv-er, (quiv-ering in) the Ri-ver Cam, They

(Call) ... (Response)
top-ple in and go for a swim, (top-pling in) the Ri-ver Cam,

(Call) ... (Response)
This is a song for the cows of the ri-ver, (graz-ing at) the Ri-ver Cam.

2.
This is a song about Justin the diver, (jumping in) the River Cam
The last time he did it he lost a fiver, (floating down) the River Cam
He took a chance and lost his dear pants, (mooning in) the River Cam
(Repeat first line)

3.
This is a song for the ghosts of the river, (haunting by) the River Cam
Don't visit at night, you might feel a quiver, (spooking by) the River Cam
[Ghostly 'oo' to the tune of the call and the response]: Oo...

4.
This is a song for the posh college rowers, (rowing down) the River cam
I think they'd look silly in feather boas, (glamorous on) the River Cam
They're earnest, sweaty, yet so refined, (sweating on) the River Cam

5.
This is a song for the ancient Green Dragon, (drinking by) the River Cam
Where Cromwell would swill his beer from a flagon, (swilling by) the River Cam
A flagon is two gallons of beer, (flagons by) the River Cam

6.
Tolkien would visit to find inspiration, (Tolkien by) the River Cam
It sparked his creative imagination, (writing by) the River Cam
The Hobbit and the Lord of the Rings, (magic by) the River Cam

7.
Metal detectorists fish for their treasure, (fishing in) the River Cam
With magnets on fishing rods at their leisure, (wishing by) the River Cam
There's bicycles, and also a pram, (cycling in) the River Cam

Seasons

"Seasons is based on fragments of memories of my life in North Cambridge, building a narrative from them of the changes within each year and across the years."

Mark is a poet, poetry promoter and event organiser in his spare time. He moved to CB4 in the early 1990s and now lives there with his wife of 21 years.

By Mark McGivern

On the last of the cold days
First buds become showers of pink and white
Milton Road's cherry blossom decoration blown
Swirled and spiralled, wind scattered
Carpets across the tarmac, a welcome mat for spring
A signal for the end of winter's short days
Hands deep in pockets, bitter winds and stinging rain
A faded memory in the first hot sunlight
Making front doors shine
More than neon Christmas colours ever could
Gardens more than pools of darkness between streetlights
Green and brown alone no more
Winter's smaller palette flooded
A feast of life bordered by wooden fences
Low brick walls, like the one, now gone
Where I used to perch on dry days and read
Opposite the Yorkshire Grey, gone too
Although the name remains to confuse tourists
I would wait there rather than walk the High Street
Walking reserved for summer nights at the Portland
After the last song, missing the last bus
Not so much fun in winter so I'd skip the shouts
Exchange "More" for the bright lights

The inside of a bus with misted windows
Like the ones I take now along the same streets
Seeing the window
My reading perch on long gone summer nights
Overlooking Green End Road
Where I'd sit on the wide inside ledge
My back against the frame
Words flowing from the page into my head
Looking up and looking out, but never down
Along the worn out pavements
Some now resurfaced but others worn and wearing out
Showing old cables put in long ago to bring
A host of channels and then access to an internet
That had just barely started
Its reach into our lives when we first met
And sat outside on summer nights
Warming with our smiles as the air cooled
The places that back then we called our own
They still remain for new lovers
Sitting where we sat
Where we still sometimes sit and talk
Of here and now like them
For the worlds not changed much more than we have
Like our streets, changing but remaining
The newest thing a prompt
Everywhere you go each new thing is yours to see
And still someone else's memory
From that bus I can see our first flat
That echoed to the clatter of a metal stair
And a door that never closed silently
I have been told it's all changed now
From there, on nights when the sun shone warm
Lighting grey walls, heavy with the golden glow
That only ever travels along the surface of the river
We would walk, not far
To a wooden table set on slightly too long grass
Between Dragon and water

By the bridge where cyclists rarely dismounted
We would sit in the last of light
And look across sun sparkling silver grey
Flowing and rippling naturally
Momentarily spattered and shattered
Oars breaking the wake of swans
Ignoring or protesting this intrusion
One became a press sensation
Before being moved to a less interruptible location
We did that too, a moving exchange of riverside
For a green space of our own
Our own bench and table, where we sit
On the very edge of the hum and rumble
In its season there is the addition of distant chants
Roars at the Abbey
The rumbling trundling hum of trains
Before they brake at our new station
In the midst of bird song
All the other life of this corner of our shared city
We while away those evenings
The ones filled with just us two, ourselves
For it's people that make a place
People who make their lives, as we make ours
Growing into it and growing in it
Through bright colours back to green and brown
Holding hands becomes hands alone
Deep in pockets against the remembered cold
I walk past the cherry trees and wait
And wait, for the blossom to begin again
Always the same and yet, like spring itself
They are also always new

75

TEAMROLLER PARK

Steamroller Park is a rap with a sung chorus by Kirsty and Rory, cousins born and raised in Cambridge. In the 80s and 90s they played on the steamroller at Steamroller Park, now known as Green End Road Park. This song explores real events and memories growing up in Cambridge across three generations. It looks at how things have changed since their childhood, and asks if life is easier or harder for kids today. The rhythms, melodic lines and harmonies that comprise the beat are presented as individual parts which are also available as samples to use for free in the GarageBand library, as named below. Performers are invited to layer, mix and match them in any order for any live or digital musical instrument to create their own unique version.

Kirsty is a nanny and Rory is a cleaner and father to two children. Both share a passion for music and recently started writing songs together.

BEAT COMPONENTS

By Kirsty Roberts and Rory Yanez

(Doghouse Melody Piano)

(Deep Electric Piano 06)

Music box, or twinkly sound.

(Drops of Rain Piano)

With chorus, tremolo and excessive reverb.

(Velvet Rope Sub Bass)

(Altered State Beat)

Drum kit   (Rim)

(Steam Machine Beat)

Drum kit (With brushes)

1.
Hi there folks, my name's Rory
And I'm about to tell you a story
I remember being in a cream stroller
Seeing kids in the park on a steamroller
But now he's older, pretending it would work
I was running over all the people that were jerks
Back when kids had imagination
You'd think silly thoughts and then just create them
Before we had a phone, street lights come on
We'd have to go and get ourselves home
If we weren't home in time, we would get grounded
Detention at home, by four walls surrounded
Everyone who's come from here
Has a house and a family, a good career
Now I'm a better man, got two kids to raise
On the same side like a parallelogram
Talking back when sweets were just a penny
We used to go and get plenty, go on a frenzy
But now I'm coming out empty
Unless it's someone else that's sent me

CHORUS

So, what's better? The past or present? When do we think life was most pleasant? Maybe things haven't got better or worse? Time may go by but it's the same universe. Maybe the past was better? Maybe the future's harder? Maybe the past was harder? Maybe the future's better?

2.
Let's take it back to the 1970s
Children had imagination, endless possibilities
No phones, high tech gadgets or technology
Kids could be kids, no fight for popularity
Our parents spent hours hanging in the fens
Making memories, laughing, building dens
Half the year spent prepping for bonfire night
Groups of young children built their own bikes
More time was spent outside than at home
Get back from school, drop your bags off and go
Pop back home when it's time to eat
Meet back up with their friends on the street
Tight knit communities, they all knew each other
All our family gathered at one table for supper
Safety was no issue, no need to lock doors
Things were so different, can't do that anymore
Back in the 70s were things better?
We think things were easier but was there less pressure?
Yes, you could get bigger, cheaper bags of sweets
But was life really any safer out on the streets?

(REPEAT CHORUS)

3.
This next verse is about my kids
So let's talk about the kinda things they did
If they could leave their technology
I'd tell them 'bout the steamroller properly
But I got no proof now that it's gone
They're on the same streets that I come from
That's why they can't leave our home
Not without their mobile phone
And not alone, they need each other
Either with their friends or with their brother
Must stay on the streets that we live
'Cos I don't trust these other kids
No staying out late at night
'Cos kids nowadays they all carry knives
When it's dark there's no street lights
So, they don't come home when the time is right
They want something from the shop 'cos they're hungry
But you can no longer get a sweet for 1p
Can't let them go with an empty tummy
So I tell them: "hurry" and give them money

OUTRO
(To be performed by a young person)
Going to the shop with some change
Also going with my mates
Even though the shop's quite long range
Quick tings before they shut the gates
Coming back with drinks while making jokes
Don't wanna think about my folks
They grew up at the park, came home after dark
Used their imagination at steamroller park

I go out with my friends 'cos I want to
I stay out late 'cos I want to
Play video games 'cos I want to
I do what I want 'cos I want to
I go out with my friends 'cos I want to
I stay out late 'cos I want to
Play video games 'cos I want to
I do what I want 'cos I want to

STRAWBERRY FAIR

This song was inspired by the community spirit behind Strawberry Fair music festival. It takes place each year on Midsummer Common, and is created by and for the people of Cambridge. Strawberry Fair is run by volunteer Strawberry Fairies who put on a show that deserves to be celebrated in a song.

Upbeat ♪♪ = ♩♪ (triplet)

By Bob Hines

(VERSE)

1. It start-ed way back in twelve-e-le-ven, it hap-pens ev-'ry year what ev-er the weath-er, Stour-bridge Fair brought traders to-geth-er, And still it's held on Mid-sum-mer Com-mon, fa-thers with their sons and moth-ers with daught-ers, it's or-gan-ised may-hem but you ought-a come a-long.

2. It's like a vil-lage green ta-ken over by hip-pies, but some are from the u-ni, some from the Ci-ty, young and old they look so pret-ty, Pa-rade round town in daz-z-ling co-lours to the vil-lage green where you'll dis-co-ver, the sweet, sweet smell of Straw-b'ry sum-mer, come a-long

3. It's ve-ry vo-lun-ta-ry for the straw-b'ry fair-ies, some are in their teens, and some in their eight-ies, com-mon folk to dig-ni-tar-ies, We've bel-ly dan-cers, lin-dy hop, hop-pers, Try as you might, you ne-ver will stop us, but here's an i-dea, come on and join us,

(REFRAIN) Straw-ber-ry Fair, Straw-ber-ry Fair, I'll be see-ing you there!

1. Yeah, yeah

to

80

[2. (BRIDGE)] (B7) there! 'Cause (F#m) lo-cal means com-mu-ni-ty, you'll find it at the heart of the fair, (B7) lo-cal means com-mu-ni-ty, (F#m) you'll see it at the heart of the fair, (B7) yeah! *TO THE START*

[3. (REFRAIN)] (B7) there! (D) Straw-ber-ry (G) Fair, (D) Straw-ber-ry (G) Fair, (B7) I'll be see-ing you there!

(VERSE 4) (E) Read all a-(E7/G#)-bout it in the (A) lo-cal pa-(A/C#)-pers, (E) bring all your (E7/G#) fa-mi-ly, (A) bring your neigh-(A/C#)-bours, a (E) free jam-bor-(E7/G#)-ee for (A) all a-(A/C#)-ges, (E) dan-cers and (E7/G#) bands are (A) gra-cing the (A/C#) sta-ges, (E) it's hap-pen-(E7/G#)-ing a-gain so (A) why are we (A/C#) wait-ing? (E) Ev-'ry-bo-(E7/G#)-dy leaves with (A) hap-py fa-(A/C#)-ces, it (E) star-ted way (E7/G#) back in (A) twelve-e-le-(A/C#)-ven and (E) hap-pens ev-'ry year what-

(REFRAIN) (B7) ev-er the weath-er it's (D) Straw - ber-ry (G) Fair, **×3** (D) Straw - ber-ry (G) Fair, (B7) I'll be see-ing you there!

(OUTRO) | (E) | (E7/G#) | (A) | (B7) | (E) | (E7/G#) | (A) | (B7) | (E) |

The Ballad of Mr Asbo

"'Mr Asbo' was an aggressive swan who made headlines in 2009 by attacking rowers on the river Cam, polarising local opinion. He was eventually moved for his own safety after attacking motorboats. I have lived in the north of Cambridge since 1985 and love the Cam towpath, but fortunately never met Mr. Asbo while walking or running there."

Stefan is a software engineer who enjoys singing and playing the guitar.

By Stefan Kaye
and Anna Hester Skelton

♩ = 96

(CHORUS)
Fours and eights and mo-tor boats, sculls, ca-noes and all that floats, I'll chase you all un-til you're gone, I'm Mis-ter As-bo the hoo-li-gan swan!

(VERSE 1)
1. While swan-ning a-long the ri-ver Cam, be-side Fen Dit-ton's shores, with my mis-sus and my cyg-nets for to see my swan-in-laws, pad-dling up to Ches-ter-ton as in a hap-py dream, when eight great oafs in a huge long boat came charg-ing down the stream. Those great big guys all in a row, with mas-sive oars, they scared us so, to stop my fa-mi-ly be-ing harmed, I flew at the one that was small and un-armed. I

[G] saved us all from [D] dreadful knocks with a [A] mighty peck in the middle of the [D] cox! **REPEAT CHORUS**

(VERSE 2)
[D] I gained a repu[A]tation as an anti[D]social bird, the [A] [G] students called me 'Stalin' and the [D] tales grew quite ab[A]surd. Some [D] called for my evic[D7]tion, but some spoke in my de[G]fence:— "The [A] swans were on the river first!" It sounded like good [D] sense. Then [Bm] Battleship Bob in his old grey barge be[F#m]came my friend and led the charge, [Bm] turned on his motor with a clank, and [A] steered his craft from bank to bank. He [G] made the oars-folk [D] look like chumps when he [A] went for a cruise in the middle of [D] The Bumps! **REPEAT CHORUS**

(VERSE 3)
[D] Then a lady called Mi[A]chelle, she came and asked [D] me what I feared. She [A] [G] whispered she'd connect with me, it [D] sounded somewhat [A] weird, but

...then I turned my anger on a motor boat or two, and the dear old Cam conservancy, they said it wouldn't do. They said that I was a splendid fella, but it's not so clever to fight a propeller. They took me off to a distant stream, I hope my kids continue the theme. As long as there are feathers on me, my own swan-song will still forever be:

REPEAT CHORUS x2

OPTIONAL LAST LINE (END)

Mister Asbo the hooligan swan!

Chorus

Fours and eights and motorboats,
Sculls, canoes and all that floats,
I'll chase you all until you're gone,
I'm Mr Asbo - the hooligan swan!

1.

While swanning along the river Cam, beside Fen Ditton's shores,
With my missus and my cygnets for to see my swan-in-laws,
Paddling up to Chesterton as in a happy dream,
When eight great oafs in a huge long boat came charging down the stream
Those great big guys all in a row, with massive oars, they scared us so,
To stop my family being harmed, I flew at the one that was small and unarmed,
I saved us all from dreadful knocks
With a mighty peck in the middle of the cox!

Chorus

2.

I gained a reputation as an anti-social bird,
The students called me 'Stalin' and the tales grew quite absurd.
Some called for my eviction, but some spoke in my defence:
"The swans were on the river first!" It sounded like good sense.
Then Battleship Bob in his old grey barge became my friend and led the charge,
Turned on his motor with a clank, and steered his craft from bank to bank.
He made the oars-folk look like chumps
When he went for a cruise in the middle of The Bumps!

Chorus

3.

Then a lady called Michelle, she came and asked me what I feared.
She whispered she'd connect with me, it sounded somewhat weird,
But then I turned my anger on a motor boat or two,
and the dear old Cam conservancy, they said it wouldn't do.
They said that I was a splendid fella, but it's not so clever to fight a propeller.
They took me off to a distant stream, I hope my kids continue the theme.
As long as there are feathers on me,
My own swansong will still forever be:

Chorus

Mr Asbo the hooligan swan!

THE GHOST OF THE SNOWCAT

"The Snowcat in north Arbury was my local as a young man in the 80s. I lived on Campkin Road, was a Labour counciller for Kings Hedges, and a teacher in Huntingdon. It was designed for Greene King by esteemed architect David Wyn Roberts and provided gravity-fed bitter from barrels in the roof space. It served the new Kings Hedges estate as a vital part of our community for many years."

Andrew is a professor at University College London, lives in Milton, and plays melodeon and Northumbrian small pipes in the Cambridge folk band Camus.

By Andrew Burn

(CHORUS)
Here's a health to the ghost of the Snow-cat. We measured our time in pints of strong ale when we were young. Here's a health to the ghost of the Snow-cat.

(VERSE)
1. On land which the Romans had named, and King Henry's Hedges had driven the game, In nineteen-fifty-nine bulldozers roared, and carved out the plan on the architect's board. Here's a

Chorus
Here's a health to the ghost of the Snowcat.
We measured our time in pints of strong ale when we were young.
Here's a health to the ghost of the Snowcat.

1.
On land which the Romans had named,
And King Henry's Hedges had driven the game.
In 1959 bulldozers roared,
And carved out the plan on the architect's board.

2.
First pub on a brand new estate,
And named for the Antarctic Sno-Cat machine.
Topped off with copper, it shines while we wait
For opening time, though we hadn't a bean.

3.
The Snowcat in Arbury Court
Was hard by the chippie and old hardware store.
Butcher and grocer, the bits that we bought
To help us to keep the bold wolf from the door.

4.
In summer when day's work was done,
We'd amble along Campkin Road for a jar.
With politics and pastimes the evenings would run
In the dim smoky light of the old public bar.

5.
But now the old pub is no more,
The ghost of the cigarette smoke, and the ale
Hangs like a mist over Arbury Court.
With sunrise the memory's soon swept away.

6.
On the skyline the copper roof soars.
The local Sikh temple now calls it their home.
Ale house to god house, it opened its doors
For people to gather wherever they roam.

The Sharing Shelf

The Sharing Shelf was set up by Simon Young in the 1990s, at the back of his workshop on Aylestone Road, north Cambridge. It lasted for nearly twenty years, and offered a space for the neighbouring community to donate and collect items for free. It divided local opinion and started to become unmanageable when much larger items, such as a fridge and bed, were donated. It is fondly remembered by local people.

Michael is based in Ely and has been writing songs for many years.

By Michael Judkins
and Anna Hester Skelton

(VERSE)

1. There was a local man called Simon Young, one of our many heroes yet unsung, to help his neighbouring community, came upon an idea of some novelty, when items seem to have no further use, not to
2. signed and built beside his old work-shop, these shelves they would encourage you to stop, with cups and saucers kettles and teapots, take one item or if you wish take lots, the popularity kept growing higher; once
3. such objection it did not defeat this kindness to be found along the street, in time a different challenge came instead, a fridge turned up, then someone brought a bed, too burdensome, he now called it a day, but for

G think of o-ther peo-ple, no ex-cuse, so
some-one brought a-long a deep fat fryer, no
near-ly twen-ty years peo-ple would say: "Just

C whe-ther you're in sick-ness or in health, please
mat-ter if you were some-one of wealth, you'd
go a-long, look round and help your-self, come

F

G come o-ver and see the shar-ing shelf.
still be wel-come at the shar-ing shelf.
take what you need from the shar-ing (TO END)

1. **C** 2. Well- shelf.
2. **C** Some

(MIDDLE 8)
F li-ving in the lo-cal neigh-bour-hood, **C** **G** ex-pressed the view the whole thing was no

C good: **C7** **F** "It lowers the tone, cre-ates a real eye-sore! **C** Take it

D7 down we don't want it a-ny more!" **G** 3. Whilst

(END)
C shelf." **F** The shar-ing shelf, **D7** the shar-ring shelf, take what you

C need **G** from the shar-ing **C** shelf.

THE SUMMER OF 1989

"This piece is inspired by a personal anecdote from my keyworker Lucy, who grew up in north Cambridge. Protests and parties are worlds apart but the political nature of raves resonate with me as I believe we need to stand together against current brutality. Lucy's story relates to my teenage years in London, falling in love and partying."

Abigail has a passion for writing, justice, change and peace. This piece expresses her ethos.

By Abigail Thorne-Miles

Booming dilapidated cars that could shake an entire skeleton
speed up the A14.
Iridescent beams light up the sky
Acid house pumps up as the yin embellishes the yang
as the night dances with
hand-me-down memories that are the late 80's.

Strawberry smoke machines
blow senses into another dimension.
Need I mention the release of souls from political tension
lingering with the sexy smell of white musk.
Raving in disorientation whilst liberating an entire nation,
falling in love
and

I think I knew love
because, that night
you became my muse and my muse you still are.
Binaural beats and the twangs of my broken guitar,
a disco light that would blind us for days
its all a haze
as I
remember the times with no complications,
burying feelings in recreation.
It all felt like a dream until you subdued me to your
fire and damnation.
I could see in your eyes that you were only morally taken
Or by someone else, apparently so God forsaken.
Our curtain came down and the circus was through.
All that was left was me you and all my tears.
So many tears

Tears of happiness for redemption
and sorrow for pain inflicted by the hierarchy
Margaret Thatcher and who's army?

Beads, peace and Osh Kosh dungarees
leather medallions swaying.
The dry hot summer of 1989
packed in love like sardines marinading in
sweat stained granddad tees
drunken apologies from a need to abolish greed.
All magazines became about teens
from top secret to front page headlines.

From Proper Stuff, Sunrise, Hacienda to the world
the Berlin Wall was knocked down
Nelson Mandela freed.
From fighters to peaceful warriors
all to the melancholic sound of Frankie Knuckle's Tears.

TURIN THE PYTHON

In June 2019, Turin the python escaped from his house on Lovell Road, Kings Hedges. His escape is one of lyricist Irene's most memorable moments as a resident of Lovell Road for over 30 years. Her brother who lives in the same road found the snake in his neighbour's tree, having had his own garden searched by police at night. This song can be performed a cappella or accompanied by piano or guitar. The snake charmer melody can be played between some or all verses. To add suspense, gradually get faster and higher, rising a semitone every couple of verses. For a super snakey rendition, emphasise the 's' sounds and invite the audience to join in with a 'Sss' when the snake charmer plays!

Irene was born in 'Old Chesterton' and is officially a 'Chestertonian'. She enjoys writing poems and short stories.

By Irene Rogers
and Emily Peasgood

(SNAKE CHARMER MELODY)
For woodwind instruments (recorder, oboe, etc.)

(VERSE)

1. Turin was a python who was restless in his bones, and so he slithered out the window of his loving home, A neighbour saw him sneaking off, they had an awful fright, The police were called and residents were woken by searchlights!

2.
Turin he was savvy as they hunted high and low
We checked under our beds, in Michael's pond, and hedgerows
My friends looked near their paddling pool and underneath the slide
But no one found where savvy, sneaky, snakey chose to hide

3.

Mister 'Snakeman' Hopkins said: "I'll travel down from Wales!
I'll help you look for Turin if you find that all else fails
But snakes are territorial and won't go very far"
Nobody in Kings Hedges dared to leave their door ajar

4.

After four long days had passed we started getting scared
Imagining a nine-foot python sliding up the stairs
We kept our windows tightly shut and locked our pets indoors
'Cause pets are tasty snacks for pythons with their giant jaws

5.

Rumours spread that pythons liked to snuggle people too
But not the kind of snuggle you'd get at the petting zoo
They wrap themselves around you and they squeeze you very tight
And when you turn a shade of blue they take a tasty bite!

6.

Turin's family worried every night and every day:
"We're sorry this has happened, it is all a big mistake!
At times he's shady, sometimes scary, but he's just a charmer
If you find him please let us know as we can keep him calmer"

7.

On day five a frightful scream was heard on Lovell Road
The sneaky snake was spotted not too far from his abode
He'd dressed in nifty camouflage to match a nearby tree
And sunbathing and sleepy, Turin smiled and looked at me
(Phew! He'd finally been found!)

8.

Turin was now famous and he made the headline news
The media took pictures and held lots of interviews
He'd seen the sights of Cambridge and was happy, safe and sound
These slippery snakeys are so cheeky when they go to ground

9.

Never lose your sneaky snake or every time you do
You'll wonder where your snake is and you'll even check the loo
The moral of this story is it's hard to trust a snake
'Cause when they need a holiday then they will just escape

UNION HOUSE

In 2016, Cambridge Adult Locality Teams mental health services moved to Union House on Union Lane, where there used to be a workhouse paid for by a local union. In this folk story a magical object causes an episode of ill health.

Connie J is a Cambridge songwriter.

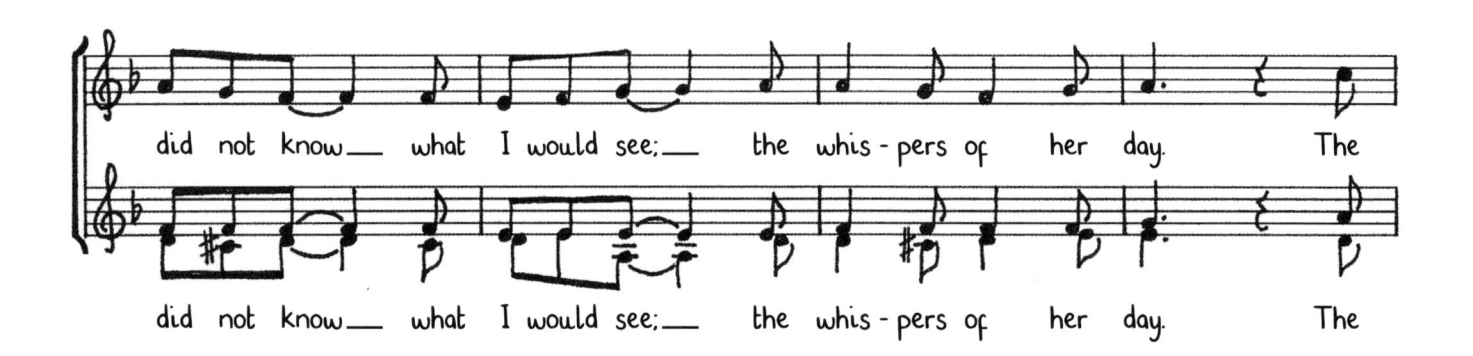

By Connie J

(VERSE 1)

I slipped in-to my mo-ther's shoes, walked a mile her way. I did not know what I would see; the whis-pers of her day. The land-scape wild, it fright-ened me; I could not un-der-stand the

terrors lurking in the hills,— the monsters shifting sand. I
terrors lurking in the hills,— the monsters shifting sand. I

(VERSE 2)
slipped in-to— my mother's shoes, I did not mean to go. The
slipped in-to— my mother's shoes, I did not mean to go. The

smell was strong, my thoughts were rushed; I could not stand the blow. The
smell was strong, my thoughts were rushed; I could not stand the blow. The

gentle hands held out to me,— the people close— beside all
gentle hands held out to me,— the people close— beside all

tried and tried to pull me out,— but I was lost inside.
tried and tried to pull me out,— but I was lost inside.

(BRIDGE)
Strip me down, make me good, find the fault in the hood. Firing's off, wiring's gone
Strip me down.   Make me good.   Find the fault.

ev'ry-thing, ev'ry-thing, ev'ry-thing might be ans-wered in U-nion House. I

In the hood. U-nion House. I

(VERSE 3)
slipped in-to my mo-ther's shoes and then slipped out once more. Bare-

slipped in-to my mo-ther's shoes and then slipped out once more. Bare-

foot-ed I could feel the grass and breathe in-to my core. She

foot-ed I could feel the grass and breathe in-to my core. She

ans-wers to me ev-'ry day in rose-ma-ry and smoke. I

ans-wers to me ev-'ry day in rose-ma-ry and smoke. I

hear her laugh with-in my own, em-braced with-in my throat.

hear her laugh with-in my own, em-braced with-in my throat.

(BRIDGE)
Strip me down, make me good, find the fault in the hood. Fi-ring's off, wi-ring's gone

Strip me down. Make me good. Find the fault.

ev'ry-thing, ev'ry-thing, ev'ry-thing might be answered in Union House.

In the hood. Union House.

ev'ry-thing, ev'ry-thing, ev'ry-thing might be answered in Union House.

Union House.

1.

I slipped into my mother's shoes, walked a mile her way.

I did not know what I would see; the whispers of her day.

The landscape wild, it frightened me; I could not understand

the terrors lurking in the hills, the monsters shifting sand.

2.

I slipped into my mother's shoes, I did not mean to go.

The smell was strong, my thoughts were rushed; I could not stand the blow.

The gentle hands held out to me, the people close beside

all tried and tried to pull me out, but I was lost inside.

Bridge

Strip me down, make me good, find the fault in the hood

Firing's off, wiring's gone, ev'rything, ev'rything, ev'rything

might be answered in Union House.

3.

I slipped into my mother's shoes and then slipped out once more.

Barefooted I could feel the grass and breathe into my core.

She answers to me ev'ryday in rosemary and smoke.

I hear her laugh within my own, embraced within my throat.

Repeat Bridge

WHEN DAISY MET WINSTON

This is a story of two people born on the same day. One enjoyed privilege, wealth and fame, whilst the other grew up as one of the workhouse poor on Union Lane in Chesterton. Fate conspired to arrange for the two to meet, and with the help of Anne Winterburn B.E.M. and Mrs Bevan of Chesterton Hospital, Daisy met Winston. This song was written with Anne's daughter Judith.

Judith moved to San Antonio, Texas in the 1960's and is a nurse.

By Judith Lamm
and Bob Hines

(VERSES 1 & 2)

1. They were both born on the same day, then their lives went ve-ry dif-fer-ent ways: One had more than he could ask for, one knocked on U-nion Road work-house door. When

2. cards on ev-'ry birth-day, in ce-le-bra-tion; they shared the same day, and she dreamed that one day they'd meet: may-be he'd be walk-ing down the street?

(PRE-CHORUS 1)

Dai-sy met Win-ston, she knew in that in-stant that this was the day she'd been wait-ing for, and when Win-ston met Dai-sy I'd like to think may-be he treat - ed her like the la - dy she was. The day Dai - sy met Win - ston. The day Dai - sy met Win - ston. 2. She sent

(VERSE 3) Work - house closed, they took down the name, Ches - ter - ton Hos - pi - tal it now be - came, and now it was Dai - sy's new home, where she was safe and with grace could grow old. The

(CHORUS) day Dai - sy met Win - ston. The day Dai - sy met Win - ston.

(VERSE 4) Fif - ty - nine, Chur - chill came to town to plant a tree in his own col - lege grounds, and now,

| G | A7 | Em7 | E7 | A | A7 |

now could it be time to take this op-por-tu-ni-ty? Mis-sus

(VERSE 5)
| D | Bm | G | A7 | D | F#7 |

Be-van___ and Anne Win-ter-burn thought Dai-sy could,

| G | A7 | D | Bm | G | A7 |

thought that she should be there,___ and by in-vi-ta-tion,

(PRE-CHORUS 2)
| Em7 | E7 | A | A7 | G | A |

Dai-sy now stood with the great and the good, and let it be writ-ten that the

| D | Bm | G | A | D | D7 |

great-est of Bri-tons bowed his head, most fit-ting, him-self lost for words, and I'm

| Gm | C7 | F | Dm | Em7 | E7 |

of the op-in-ion, you can take it as a gi-ven, that proud old wo-man was

(PRE-CHORUS 1)
| A | A7 | G | A | D | Bm |

once more a girl. When Dai-sy met Win-ston, I swear in that in-stant that

| G | A | D | D7 | Gm | C7 |

this was the day she'd wait-ed for, and when Win-ston met Dai-sy I'd *like to think may-be he treat-ed her like the la-dy she was. The*

(CHORUS)
day Dai-sy met Win-ston. The day Dai-sy met Win-ston.

(VERSE 6)
When they died still they shared the same day: one a state fu-ne-ral, one un-marked grave. They lie in dig-ni-ty: West-min-ster Ab-bey, Ches-ter-ton Ce-me-try. The

(CHORUS)
day Dai-sy met Win-ston. The day Dai-sy met Win-ston.

WHEN JONNY PLAYS

"Jon Ward has been an integral part of the Cambridge music scene since the 70s. I have often played folk music with him at The Carlton Arms; from his many bands to DJ sets, he brings a smile wherever he goes."

Zoë is a primary school teacher in Cambridgeshire and before that worked extensively as a music tutor and community musician throughout Cambridgeshire and Peterborough.

By Zoë Austin

(VERSE 1)

They say a place is made up by its peo-ple; not build-ings, roads or un-der-pass sub-ways, but by folk like Jon-ny, born and bred in Cam-bridge, who lights up a-ny room when he plays. When

(CHORUS)

Jon-ny plays we all start smi-ling. When Jon-ny plays we put a-way sad things. There's ma-gic in his mu-sic and there's heart in his strings, when Jon-ny plays the whole world sings. When Jon-ny plays the whole world sings.

(VERSE 2)

mu-sic man, he al-ways a-ma-zes, A-ny plucked string beast is his to tame, They fill up all his heart and his at-ten-tion, and they fill up his home just the same. When

(VERSE 3)
No need for paper notes, he's got his tunes safe, Stored in music memory so wide. Rock 'n' roll, blues, folk and country, He plays them all, no need to special-ise When

(VERSE 4)
Red boots, a baseball cap, jeans and a T-shirt, Silver round his neck and in each ear, A jewel blue trike to tour the by-ways, A teenage heart to stem the creeping years. When

(VERSE 5)
A thousand, thousand gigs across the decades, A billion of his chords still skip in space, His notes have graced so many local ears, His music serves to sancti-fy this place. When

ACKNOWLEDGEMENTS

Songs and Verses from North Cambridge was commissioned by Brookgate and Network Rail with the assistance of Commission Projects and Chesterton Community College. It would not have been possible without contributions from people in the local community:

SPECIAL THANKS TO:

The children of Chesterton Community College for the decorative alphabet and numbers that feature throughout the book: Amelia Wood, Annabel Aston, Bea Campbell, Carrie Davis, Cayley Neufeld, Danny Standring, Edie Donoghue, Eleanor Hodgson, Emilija Agniete Noreikaite, Fergus Green, Gabriella Giussani, Joanna Yung, Jonny Storey, Imogen Hewlett, Isobel Widmer, Katy Whitelaw, Liam Grogan Weyman, Lorenzo Lucamarini, Louis Bardes, Marnie Pounds, Max Maddox, Mia Chong, Portia Drewry, Rachel Treece, Rebecca Jameson and Yinghan Ho.

Residents past and present for contributing songs, poems, ideas, stories and time: Abigail Thorne-Miles, Andrew Burn, Anna Shelton, Caroline Mead, Chiara Berry, Chloe Floyd, Connie J, Daniel Nestlerode, Darren Fitzpatrick, Deborah Slee, Eleana Ray, Genevieve Berry, George Bacon, Guy Dinwiddy, Irene Rogers, Jessica Law, Judith Lamm, Kirsty Roberts, Lara Gisborne, Liz Huelin, Lucille Rococoa, Maira Kay, Mark McGivern, Michael Judkins, Neil Banks, Nicky Floyd, Rory Yanez, Sharon Sullivan, Stefan Kaye, Zoë Austin and all who contributed ideas anonymously.

Mural Artists who inspired Kindness is Always in Season: Dan Biggs, Sa'adiah Khan and Samirah Khan.

GRATEFUL THANKS TO THE TEAM:
Lead artist & composer: Emily Peasgood
Songwriter: Anna Hester Skelton
Songwriter: Bob Hines
Illustration & typesetting: Danielle Woolley
Assistant: Connor Sansby
Videographer: Robert Hill
Book printer: Ex Why Zed

FOR SUPPORT IN THE COMMUNITY:
Black Fen Folk Club: David Savage
Cambridge City Council: Akua Obeng-Frimpong and Binnie Pickard
Cambridge Folk Club: Andy Treby, Calvin Monk, Marion Treby and Robin Mansfield
Cambridgeshire Library Service: Nikki Cooper
Chesterton Community College: Catherine Wilson and Morgain Murray Williams
Kettle's Yard: Karen Thomas
Museum of Cambridge: Florencia Nannetti
SIN Cru: James Therobot and Lucille Rococoa

SPECIAL THANKS TO:
Alan Barrett, David Wright, Grace Thorne, Jim Butler, Matt Kelly, Martin Carthy, Mike Northern, Sarah Coxson and Sarah Venn.

THE SONGWRITING TEAM

EMILY PEASGOOD

Emily is an Ivors Composer Award winning composer and sound artist who creates research-led and site-specific interactive artworks for galleries and outdoor public spaces, ranging from large-scale community events to intimate sound installations. Her work invites people to connect with people and places that are forgotten, taken for granted, or surrounded by histories that can be remembered and celebrated through sound and music. Peasgood is best known for her work creating outdoor artworks and community projects.

www.emilypeasgood.com

ANNA HESTER SKELTON

Anna is a singer-songwriter, a teacher and a huge believer in the power of the arts to connect people and share stories. She has released two EPs and her first album, Postcard Songs, will be released in 2021. The songs on the album all use postcards as a starting point, and tell a range of intertwining stories inspired by the people and places the postcards depict. As well as being a musician, Anna is a teacher with a range of experience within English as a Second Language, singing and songwriting, and Special Educational Needs and Disabilities. Anna delivered a TEDx talk in 2018 about embracing your creativity called 'You can make it'. Although Anna wasn't born in Cambridge, she feels at home there. Her parents met when they were both working at Heffers Bookshop and her grandmother lived in Cambridge, so she visited regularly and later attended Cambridge University.

www.annahester.com

BOB HINES

Bob has been a Water Consultant for over 30 years but his real passion is music, in any shape, form or variety. He has been writing songs for over 40 years and has an interest in songs that are written about local areas and communities. One of his many albums, Songs from The Priory (2015), is a collection of his songs about his home town of St Neots where he helps to run St Neots Folk Club. Bob is a self-taught and prolific songwriter who taught himself guitar when he was 14 so he could join a glam rock bank. From there came heavy metal, Motown, rock, jazz, a little classical, country, an Open University Music Degree and finally folk music. Bob has played at The Cambridge Folk Festival and most of the clubs and pubs in and around Cambridge.

A
A
A
A
B
B
THE BIG ISSUE!
B
B
B
B
C
C
C
D
E
F
FEN ROAD
G
REEN END ROAD
G
G
H
H
I
J
K

With special thanks to the children of Chesterton Community College.

LICENCE

1. Save for all and any moral rights and conditional on every copy of any work from Songs and Verses from North Cambridge ("the Book") reproducing the notice of assertion of moral right of paternity ("the Notice"), identifying the author of the work, as it is set out below, to the extent possible under law, Emily Peasgood waives all of her copyright and related rights to the book.

The Notice: "The right of [author] to be identified as the author of [name of the work] has been asserted in accordance with the Copyright, Designs and Patents Act 1998, sections 77 and 78".

2. For the avoidance of doubt copyright in the following works does not belong to Emily Peasgood and has not been waived by the copyright holders: (i) G.O.A.T. by Lucille Rococo; (ii) Green End Road by George Bacon.

3. This work is published from: England and Wales.

Statement of purpose
4. Emily Peasgood wishes to permanently relinquish the rights set out below in relation to the Book for the purpose of contributing to a commons of creative, cultural and scientific works that the public can reliably and without fear of later claims of infringement build upon, modify, incorporate in other works, reuse and redistribute as freely as possible in any form whatsoever and for any purposes, including commercial purposes.

Waiver
5. To the greatest extent permitted by, but not in contravention of, applicable law, Emily Peasgood hereby overtly, fully, permanently and irrevocably, waives, abandons, and surrenders, save for moral rights, all of her Copyright and Related Rights, and associated claims and causes of action, whether now known or unknown (including existing as well as future claims and causes of action), in the Book (i) in all territories worldwide, (ii) for the maximum duration provided by applicable law or treaty (including future time extensions), (iii) in any current or future medium and for any number of copies, and (iv) for any purpose whatsoever, including without limitation commercial, advertising or promotional purposes, conditional on every copy of any work from the Book reproducing the notice of assertion of moral right of paternity, identifying the author of the work (the "Waiver"). Emily Peasgood makes the Waiver for the benefit of each member of the public at large and to the detriment of her heirs and successors, fully intending that such Waiver shall not be subject to revocation, rescission, cancellation, termination, or any other legal or equitable action to disrupt the quiet enjoyment of the Book by the public as contemplated by her express Statement of Purpose.

6. Should any part of the Waiver for any reason be judged legally invalid or ineffective under applicable law, then the Waiver shall be preserved to the maximum extent permitted taking into account Emily Peasgood's express Statement of Purpose. In addition, to the extent the Waiver is so judged, Emily Peasgood hereby grants to each affected person a royalty-free, non transferable, non sublicensable, non exclusive, irrevocable Licence to exercise her Copyright and Related Rights in the Book (i) in all territories worldwide, (ii) for the maximum duration provided by applicable law or treaty (including future time extensions), (iii) in any current or future medium and for any number of copies, and (iv) for any purpose whatsoever, including commercial, advertising or promotional purposes (the "License"), conditional on every copy of any work from the Book reproducing the notice of assertion of moral right of paternity, identifying the author of the work. The Licence shall be deemed effective as of 1 April 2021. Should any part of the Licence for any reason be judged legally invalid or ineffective under applicable law, such partial invalidity or ineffectiveness shall not invalidate the remainder of the License, and in such case Emily Peasgood hereby affirms that she will not (i) exercise any of his or her remaining Copyright and Related Rights in the Book, save for those reserved by this Licence or (ii) assert any associated claims and causes of action with respect to the Book, in either case contrary to this license.

7. Emily Peasgood disclaims responsibility for clearing the right of other persons that may apply to the Book or any use thereof, including without limitation any person's Copyright and related rights in the Book or parts thereof. She further disclaims responsibility for obtaining any necessary consents, permissions or other rights required for any use of the Book or parts thereof.

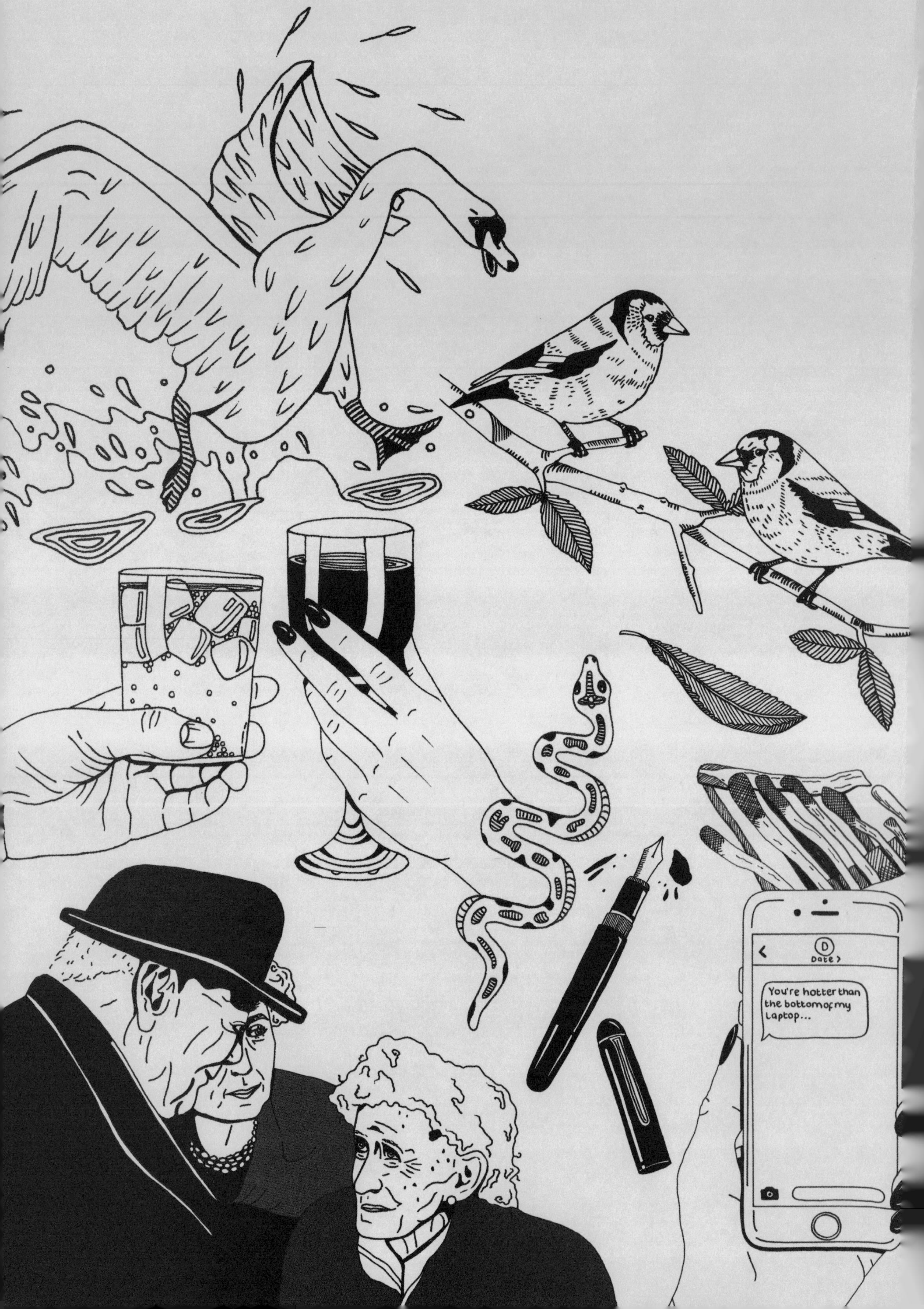
D
Date >
You're hotter than the bottom of my Laptop...

LOCUS IN DOMOS LOCI POPULUM!

WORDS AND MUSIC BY BOB HINES AND EMILY PEASGOOD

Inspired by events in Waterstreet, Cambridge, 2017

Public Domain, 2021

LOCUS IN DOMOS

This is a tale of local folks' struggle with ever-rising house prices in Cambridge. When someone responded with a very 'Cambridge' protest - graffiti in Latin - grammatical errors were analysed and discussed in the press by academics at Cambridge University. After all, in Cambridge that's how it's done!

By Bob Hines and Emily Peasgood

66 bpm

(Guitar)

1. His

(VERSE)

1. lo - cal was the Pike and Eel, it was his se-cond home, 'til the
2. so he went in the dead of night; he went to 'Mil-lion-aire Row', with a

land was sold and in its place they built a 'Mil-lion-aire Row'. 'Re -
spray can and the cause to fight the fight for lo - cal homes, New

flec - tions' was the build-ings' name, (where the posh drink Char-don-nay), 'twas
hou - ses sprayed with La-tin text di-vi-ded Town and Gown, the

priced so high and far be-yond what lo - cal folks could pay.
scho - lars cried: "What-ev-er next?" For gram-mat-i-cal er-rors were found!

(CHORUS)

Lo - cus in do - mos, lo - ci pop - u - lum,

where graf - fi - ti is in La - tin, in Cam-bridge that's how it's

done, where graf - fi - ti is in La - tin, in Cam-bridge that's how it's

(VERSE)

done. (Guitar)   2. And 3. When

pric-es drive folks a-way, and they're high-er ev-'ry day, no

lo-cal homes for lo-cal folk,_ what else can you say,_____ but

(CHORUS) [x3]

Lo-cus in do-mos, lo-ci pop-u-lum,

where graf-fi-ti is in La-tin,_ in Cam-bridge that's how it's

done,____ where graf-fi-ti is in La-tin,_ in Cam-bridge that's how it's

done. (Guitar)   that's how it's   A place for

(OUTRO) [Vamp]

homes,_____ A place for peo— —ple. A place for

(END)

homes,_____ in Cam-bridge that's how it's done

Songs and Verses from North Cambridge

Typesetting and Illustration by Danielle Woolley

The one that got away